Richard Sorger/Jenny Udale

The Fundamentals
of Fashion Design

2nd
edition

ava
academia

Contents

3 Fabrics and techniques

4 Construction

5 Developing a collection

Introduction

Oscar Wilde, in his infamously satirical style, once claimed that: 'Fashion is merely a form of ugliness so unbearable that we are compelled to alter it every six months.' Oscar Wilde was passionate about his appearance and his clothes, so there's little doubt that he made this remark with his tongue planted firmly in his cheek. Wilde's statement does make a useful point, however, about how we are all drawn to fashion, not only as a means to individually express ourselves through the way in which we choose to dress, but also as a means of creative expression through design.

Fashion is a constant search for the new. It is hungry and ruthless. To be able to create clothes is also very exciting and very rewarding. But designers do not just sit at a desk and design pretty frocks. They need to research and develop a theme, source fabrics and develop a cohesive range with them. A good designer understands the differing properties of fabric and what is achievable with them, so an understanding of the techniques of garment construction is essential to fashion design. When developing a collection, a designer needs to think about who they are designing for, what type of garments they are developing and for what season.

In this completely revised and updated second edition, we will introduce you to the fundamental principles of fashion design, so that you can begin thinking about these things in relation to your own design work. We have introduced case studies at the end of each chapter in order to examine the work of a particular designer in relation to the topics that we've explored within that chapter. We have also included some chapter-specific exercises that will enable you to put into practice the ideas that you have read about. Exciting new interviews with industry professionals are also peppered throughout the book, to provide you with insights into what it really means to have a career in fashion; which we hope will motivate you in your design work and inspire you as you embark on your own career within the industry.

We hope that you enjoy it…

1

1–4 **Bronwen Marshall**

Menswear outfits from Bronwen Marshall's graduation collection, which formed part of her MA Fashion course at the Royal College of Art, London.

2

3

4

1 Research

No good design can happen without some form of research taking place. In terms of design, 'research' means the creative investigation of visual or literary references that will inspire and inform your designs. The first thing that any designer will do is to undertake some form of research; but all designers will have their own particular approach to how they carry this out.

As a fledgling designer, clothes cannot be designed without researching and understanding clothes that already exist. A designer needs to be aware of the different types of garments, details and the techniques used to create those garments in order to create their own designs. (For example, there are many different types of pockets, collars and stitches used to make and decorate clothes and the use of these details within a design will make a huge difference to the overall look of a garment.) As a designer, you also need to be informed about the work of other designers, past and present.

But as well as knowing about and understanding clothes, and being aware of the work of other fashion designers, a designer also needs to create something new – so they will often research a 'theme' or 'concept' as a way of keeping the work original.

Are you fashionable?

There is no point in trying to be fashionable. This book cannot tell you how to design fashion; it can only tell you what the ingredients are, ways to put them together, and many of the important things that you will need to consider when designing clothes. Clothing is only 'fashionable' when your peers or the industry deem a design to be of the zeitgeist. It either is or it isn't.

The Oxford English Dictionary defines fashion as 'a popular or the latest style of clothing, hair, decoration or behaviour'. Essentially, it means a style that is up-to-date, and how this is agreed upon is subjective and relies on a number of factors. For instance, the punk movement was a reflection of how many young people were feeling in the late 1970s – disenchanted with the politics and culture of the time – and was somewhat engineered by Malcolm McLaren and designer Vivienne Westwood. Not that the punk movement set out to be 'fashionable' – anything but! Its aim was to be peripheral, subversive. But this reinforces the idea that trying too hard should not be a factor.

Exhibitions, films and music can have a huge influence on what is deemed fashionable at a given time.

For fashion design, it is important to develop an awareness of your own taste and style (not how you dress, as designers are not always concerned with dressing in the latest trends; as a designer, you almost have permission not to worry about how you dress as you are doing such a good job of dressing others in your day job!).

Not everyone has an aptitude or desire to design 'unconventional' clothes. Some designers focus on the understatement or detail of garments. Other designers may design 'conventional' garments, but it is the way that they are put together, or styled, that ultimately makes an outfit original and modern. Knowing what you are best at is essential, but this doesn't mean that you shouldn't experiment. It can take a while to 'know yourself' – and this period of discovery is usually spent at college. There has to be a certain amount of soul-searching involved; it's not so much about becoming the designer that you want to be, but rather about discovering the designer that you are.

You must be true to your own vision of how you want to dress someone. Beyond that, the rest is in the hands of the industry and the fashion-buying public to decide, and for every person who likes your work, there will always be someone who simply doesn't. This is to be expected, and working in such a subjective field can sometimes be confusing; but eventually you will learn to navigate your way through criticism and either develop a steely exterior or recognize which opinions you really respect and which you ought to simply disregard. Once you accept this situation, you will be free to get on with what you are best at – designing clothes.

1 **Vivienne Westwood**
Vivienne Westwood wearing her 'Destroy' T-shirt.

1

'You have a vocabulary of ideas which you have to add and subtract in order to come up with an equation right for the times.'

Vivienne Westwood

Know your subject

Finding out about designers, past and present, is the first essential bit of research that you will undertake. If a career in fashion is what you want, then you really need to know your subject. This might appear to be an obvious statement, but it needs to be said. You may protest, 'but I don't want to be influenced by other designers' work'. Of course not, but unless you know what has preceded you, how do you know that you aren't naively reproducing someone else's work? Most designers get into fashion because they are passionate about clothes – fanatical even. This hunger and excitement for clothes doesn't disappear when you become an established designer either; a career in fashion is also about a certain level of curiosity and competitiveness with your peers.

Making yourself 'fashion aware' doesn't happen overnight – but if you're genuinely passionate about the subject, it is natural to want to find out about it (that's why you've picked up this book, after all). If you're applying to a university or college to study fashion, your interview panel will want you to demonstrate that you have a rudimentary knowledge of designers and their styles. You may even be asked who you like and dislike in order to give you an opportunity to display your knowledge and justify your answer.

Magazines are a good place to start, but don't just automatically reach for the big players like 'Elle' and 'Vogue'. There are many more magazines out there, each appealing to a different niche market and style subculture, and you should gain knowledge of as many as possible; they are all part of the fashion machine. Think about who the magazine's target audience is as this is an important factor when deciding if it is relevant to you and your lifestyle (for example, is it aspirational?).

Magazines will not only make you aware of different designers, but so-called lifestyle magazines will also make you aware of other design industries and cultural events that often influence (or will be influenced by) fashion. By regularly reading magazines, you will also become aware of stylists, journalists, fashion photographers and hair and make-up artists, models, muses, brands and shops that are all-important to the success of a fashion designer.

There are some great websites that show images of the catwalk collections almost as soon as the show has taken place, such as www.vogue.com and www.style.com. There are also many independent blogs on the Internet posted up by amateurs writing passionately about fashion, free of the constraints of advertisers. You might find it interesting to follow some of the blogs you discover, as it's always worth hearing another opinion.

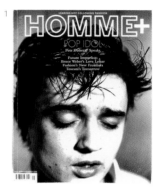

1–15 **Magazines**
There are a number of fashion and lifestyle magazines that you can refer to which can inform and inspire your own work.

< Are you fashionable?
Know your subject
Starting your research >

Starting your research

Designers are like magpies, always on the look out for something to use or steal! Fashion moves incredibly fast compared to the other creative industries and it can feel like there is constant pressure to reinvent the wheel each season. Designers need to be continually seeking new inspiration in order to keep their work fresh and contemporary, and above all, to keep themselves stimulated. In this sense, research means creative investigation, and good design can't happen without some form of research. It feeds the imagination and inspires the creative mind.

Research takes two forms. One kind is sourcing material and practical elements. Many fledgling designers forget that finding fabrics and other ingredients – rivets, fastenings or fabric treatments, for example – must make up part of the process of research. Having an appreciation of what is available, from where, and for how much, is essential.

The other form of research is the kind you do once you've decided on a theme or concept for use in your designs. Themes can be personal, abstract or more literal. Alexander McQueen, Vivienne Westwood and John Galliano have designed collections where the sources of inspiration are clear to see.

McQueen's Spring/Summer 2010 collection 'Plato's Atlantis' (his last), displayed a strong reptilian influence, in both the digital prints featured in his designs and the appearance of the models. The concept behind the collection was that just as humankind evolved from the sea, so might we be heading back to an underwater world in the future as a consequence of the ice cap dissolving.

Westwood has drawn on themes such as pirates, the paintings of Fragonard and seventeenth- and eighteenth-century decorative arts in the Wallace Collection for inspiration in different collections. Galliano has been influenced by the circus, ancient Egypt, punk singer Siouxsie Sioux and the French Revolution.

Designers may also convey a mood or use a muse for inspiration. Both McQueen and Galliano have based collections on the Marchesa Luisa Casati, for instance (see page 34). Another of McQueen's muses was the late magazine editor, Isabella Blow. He dedicated two shows to her, the first when she was alive (Autumn/Winter 2006–07's 'The Widows of Culloden') and the Spring/Summer 2008 show 'La Dame Bleue' after her death in 2007.

Using a theme or concept makes sense because it will hold together the body of work, giving it continuity and coherence. It also sets certain boundaries – which of course the designer is free to break – but having a theme initially gives the designer focus.

Choosing a theme or concept

When choosing a theme or concept, be honest. It needs to be something that you can work and live with for the duration of the collection. This means that it should be a subject that you are interested in, that stimulates you and that you understand.

A theme can loosely be defined as a visual or literary reference that will directly influence the look of the clothes. The references made to the theme in the clothes can sometimes be very literal if, for example, your designs are based on Russian constructivism; or the references could be more obscure and only make sense to you, the designer.

A concept is a methodology that informs how clothes are designed. For example, you could aim to express a sense of isolation through the clothing and in terms of how the user will feel when wearing the clothes.

Either of these approaches is appropriate and it is about choosing which method works best for you. But it does need to work for you; it is pointless choosing a theme or concept that doesn't inspire you. If the ideas are still struggling to come after a certain time, a clever designer will be honest and seriously question their choice of theme/concept.

Remember: press and buyers are generally only interested in the outcome. Do the clothes look good? Do they flatter? Do they excite? Will they sell? They are not necessarily interested in how well you've managed to express quantum physics through a jacket. But if this is what you want to express, then do it. Other people, such as stylists and art directors, however, will be very interested in the story behind your designs, and your theme/concept can thus also work as a way of reeling in interested parties.

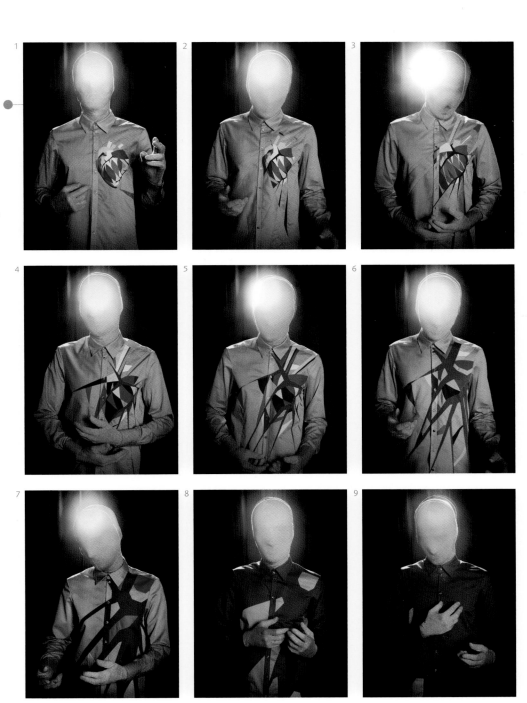

1–9 Heart shirts

These shirts by Bronwen Marshall were inspired by a Paul Simon lyric from his song 'Graceland' (…'losing love/ Is like a window in your heart/ And everybody sees you're blown apart'). The heart-shape fragments and disperses across the nine shirts.

In fashion:
John-Gabriel Harrison

Why did you choose to pursue menswear as opposed to womenswear?

I chose menswear initially because I wanted to make clothes for myself. I am very interested in details and finishings, and menswear allows me to exercise this interest.

Please describe the philosophy behind your design work

My focus is really on the details and quality. I want my clothes to be (easily) wearable and discreet, but constructed in an obsessive (and hopefully interesting) way. I don't particularly care for details in menswear that are decorative; I believe that they should be functional. For me, the greatest pleasure in wearing clothes is that of discovering new details over time and use, and I would like this to be reflected in the way I approach my own design. There is something quite satisfying about wearing a piece of clothing that is discreet and classic, and only you know all of its intricacies. I suppose in this sense, I design for somebody who is not looking to make a big statement, but is more concerned with quality and functionality.

What role does research have in your design practice? Do you enjoy doing research?

I find research is often the most exciting part of the process. I spend a lot of time collecting vintage garments and photographing them, and am trying to build up a library of images that I can always come back to. I recently had a phase of collecting early twentieth-century European nightshirts; I have almost 10 now! It's amazing to see the differences in how they were constructed. Some (which I imagine belonged to wealthier people) are entirely stitched by hand; others are far cruder in their construction (but are equally useful for details to reference).

What do you look for in a theme or concept? What ingredients does a theme or concept need in order to inspire/provoke your design ideas?

I tend to avoid sticking to themes too much. I normally like to design a wardrobe, rather than anything too specific. That being said, there will normally be something, often a film, or a particular book, that will dictate a mood or even a key look. I don't think that there is anything specific in a theme that I look for.

What inspires you?

All sorts of things! I watch a lot of films, so often I'll be inspired by perhaps a general mood or colours, or sometimes something far more specific. The way in which a character wears something, or a particular garment.... Equally, I can get really excited by somebody I pass in the street or see on a bus. London is particularly good for spotting interesting looking people. I think a lot of people are inspired by the way in which young people dress here, but I often find older, probably retired men equally interesting, there's something about the relaxed way in which they dress.

What is your approach to research? Is it an organic process of gathering references or do you have an idea for a theme and gather research accordingly?

My process is generally quite organic. When I start researching, I tend to try and watch as many films and visit as many exhibitions as possible, and take whatever I can from them. I then spend a good while in the library looking at photography books, old fashion and art magazines, as well as anything more specific, and start to work out the direction I want to take. During this whole time, I am always looking for interesting vintage garments for details and shapes. Once I have a fairly clear idea of where I'm going, I look more carefully at fabrics.

Fashion file

I grew up in Cambridge with an English father and a French mother. I decided to pursue fashion quite late during my art foundation course, after seeing Hedi Slimane's early Dior Homme collections. I spent a total of three years at Middlesex University in London and took a year out before my final year to be the sole assistant to the menswear designer at Mulberry. Whilst in my final year, I had friends on the MA Fashion course at Central Saint Martins, London, UK, who recommended the course to me and so I decided that I had to do the MA Fashion course.

What do you actually do with your research while you are working with it? And what do you do with it when you have finished using it?

I tend to keep a digital record of all the research garments that I have collected. I then print these out and keep them together with all of my other photocopies (from books and magazines). I also sometimes scan pieces of garments directly, as this can show details, particularly stitching, really clearly. I sketch on loose sheets of paper and keep them in rough piles. After I have a fairly clear idea of the direction that I'm heading in, I try to arrange my research and sketches into some kind of logical, readable order. Often a page of design will be followed by key images of research, or more detailed sketches.

< Starting your research
In fashion: John-Gabriel Harrison
Sources of research >

1–3 John-Gabriel Harrison Looks from John-Gabriel Harrison's graduation Autumn/Winter 2012 collection as part of his MA Fashion course at Central Saint Martins, London.

How do you approach the design – after the research is complete or during?

I keep all my research and design work on loose sheets until quite late on, so that things can be edited and rearranged as much as possible. It's useful to have this flexibility of seeing everything together while things are still being developed. I sketch onto white A4 copy paper (8.3 x 11.7 inches), and when I start making toiles, I draw over photos from the fittings.

Is there a pattern to how you design?

I don't really follow a pattern in terms of where or when I design. I spend time either at home or in the studio sketching, often with relevant research (images, garments, details) laid out in front of me. Most of my ideas come to me at inappropriate times; in bed, on the bus, at work, so I'll scrawl a sketch and some notes onto whatever's at hand, then work on it more thoroughly when I can.

Do you prefer to design in 2D, 3D or a combination of both?

I enjoy both 2D and 3D ways of working. I don't drape on the stand and tend to have a fairly clear idea of how something will be before I start making toiles. I do however make up lots of samples for details/stitches/fabric washes and so on during the designing process. This is an aspect of 3D work that I particularly enjoy.

When you have finished designing what happens then?

I tend to continue designing throughout the toiling process, often drawing over and over photocopies of photographs from toile fittings. I am really fortunate to get to work with great pattern cutters on the MA at Central Saint Martins, so they often work on the more complex patterns with me. I always sew all of the toiles myself, and sometimes use a machinist to sew some of my final samples.

Which part of creating a collection, from beginning to end, do you enjoy the most and why?

I would say that the research stages are the most exciting. It's a really exciting feeling to stumble across a great image or garment, sometimes to the point of being overwhelming. I also enjoy the development and construction stages a lot, but find them slower and sometimes more frustrating (if things don't go to plan!).

Sources of research

Where you go to begin your research depends on your theme or concept. For an enquiring designer, the act of researching is like detective work, hunting down elusive information and subject material that will ignite a spark.

The easiest place to start your research is on the Internet. The World Wide Web is a fantastic source of images and information. However, the Internet tends to have a little information about a lot of subjects and so it should never be relied upon as the only resource for information. The Internet is also useful for sourcing manufacturers, fabrics or companies that produce specialist materials or that perform specific services.

A good library is a treasure. Local libraries are geared to provide books to a broad cross-section of the community, so tend to have a few books about many subjects. Specialist libraries are the most rewarding, and the older the library the better – books that are long out of print will (hopefully) still be on the shelves, or at least viewable upon request. Colleges and universities should have a library geared towards the courses that are being taught, though access may be restricted if you are not actually studying there. Start collecting your own books to form your own library. You don't need to spend a fortune on lots of books; some books will be invaluable and you will return to use them again and again. Art galleries often have excellent bookshops too.

1

1 **Balmain**
From the military-inspired Balmain Spring/ Summer 2009 collection.

Flea markets and antique fairs are useful sources of inspirational objects and materials for designers. It goes without saying that clothing of any kind, be it antique or contemporary, can inspire more clothes. Historic, ethnic or specialist clothing – military garments, for example – offer insight into details, methods of manufacture and construction that you may not have encountered before.

Like flea markets, charity shops are great places to find clothes, books, records and bric-a-brac that, in the right hands and with a little imagination, could prove inspirational. Everyday objects that are no longer popular or are perceived as kitsch can be appropriated, rediscovered and used ironically to design clothes.

National museums, such as London's Victoria and Albert Museum or New York's Metropolitan Museum of Art, not only collect and showcase interesting objects from around the world, both historical and contemporary, but also have an excellent collection of costumes that can be viewed upon request.

Large companies with available budgets send their designers on research trips, often abroad, to search for inspiration. Designers are armed with a research budget and a camera, and are instructed to record and buy anything that might prove useful for the coming (or future) season.

Some sources of research images are photocopies, postcards, photographs and tear sheets from magazines and drawings. But anything can be used for research: images, fabrics, details such as buttons or an antique collar – anything that inspires you qualifies as research. Whatever you collect as part of your research needs to be within easy reach (and view), so that you have your references constantly around you; the more you see a reference, the more it will make you think. Look often at your research and analyse what you like and why you collected it.

2

2 **Vivienne Westwood**
Vivienne Westwood researched the cut of pirate clothing for her Pirate Collection Autumn/Winter 1981–82.

3 **Pirates**
Pirates could prove a good starting point for your research.

4 **Military clothing**
Some examples of military costume – a potential source of inspiration.

3

4

1

1 **Research**
Pages from a research sketchbook.

The research book

As a designer, you will eventually develop an individual approach to 'processing' your research. Some designers collect piles of photocopies and fabrics that find their way onto a wall in the studio. Others compile research books or sketchbooks where images, fabrics and trimmings are collected and collated, recording the origin and evolution of a collection. Still others take the essence of the research and produce what are called mood-, theme- or storyboards.

A research book is not necessarily solely for the designer's use. Showing research to other people is useful when trying to convey the themes or concepts of a collection. It might be used to communicate your theme or concept to your tutor, your employers, employees or a stylist.

Research books are not just scrapbooks. A scrapbook implies that the information is collected, but unprocessed. There is nothing duller than looking through pages of lifeless, rectangular images that have been (too) carefully cut out. It is also debatable how much a designer gleans from creating pages like this. A research book should instead reflect the thought processes and personal approach taken to a project. It becomes more personal when it is drawn on and written in, and when the images and materials that have been collected are manipulated or collaged.

Collage

The word 'collage' is derived from the French word 'colle', meaning 'glue'. A good collage is created when the separate elements (images) work on different levels, to form both a whole and the individual component parts of the image created at the same time. Successful collages usually include a bricolage of different-sized, differently sourced images that provide a stimulating visual rhythm.

2

2 **Research**
A page from a research sketchbook.

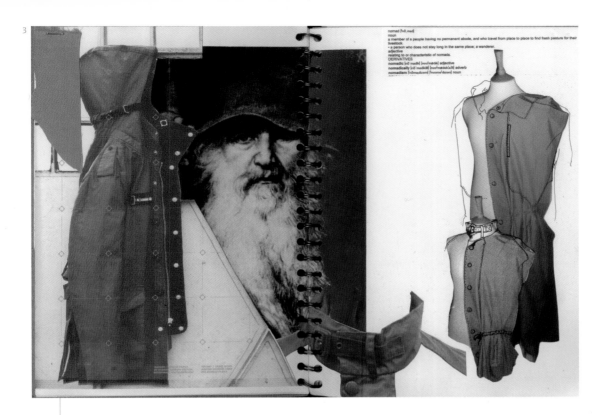

3–5 **Collages**

Examples of collages and drawings from research sketchbooks.

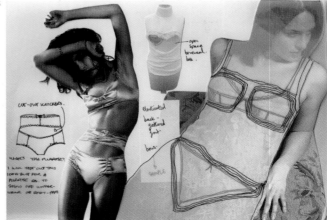

6

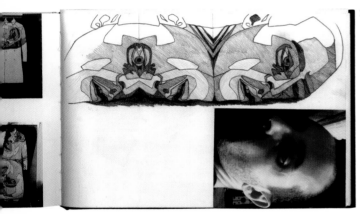

7

Drawing

Drawing a part or the whole of a picture you have collected as research helps you to understand the shapes and forms that make up the image, which in turn enables you to appreciate and utilize the same curve in a design or when cutting a pattern.

Using collage and making your own drawings allows you to deconstruct an image, such as a photograph, photocopy, drawing or postcard. This is necessary because it may not be the whole image that will ultimately be useful to your designs; a picture may have been chosen for its 'whole', but it is only when it has been examined in more depth that other useful elements may be discovered. For example, a photograph of a gothic cathedral is rich in decorative flourishes, but you almost need a magnifying glass to be able to appreciate the intricate detail it contains.

By cutting up an image or using a 'viewfinder' – a rectangle paper 'frame' that enables you to focus on part of an image, much like the viewfinder on a camera – smaller elements or details can become more apparent and so be more easily examined.

8

6–8 **Analytical drawing**
Some striking examples of drawings from research sketchbooks.

< Sources of research
The research book
Mood-, theme- and storyboards >

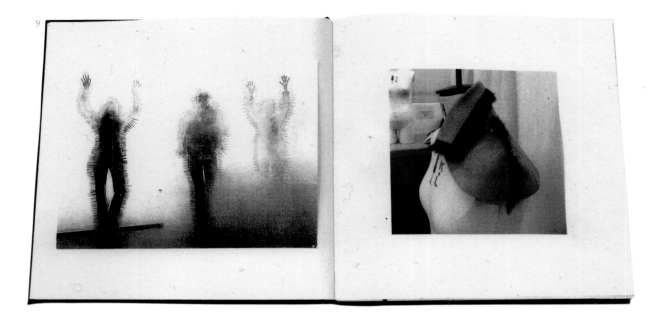

9

10

Juxtaposition

Placing images and fabrics together on the pages of your research book will help you to make important decisions about the content of your designs. Sometimes disparate images or materials may share similarities even though they are essentially different. For example, the spiral shape of an ammonite fossil is similar to a spiral staircase or a rosette. Or an image may be suggestive of a fabric you have sourced – for example, a piece of devoré velvet may evoke the texture of moss.

By utilizing drawing, collage and juxtaposition in your research books, you are processing and analysing what has been collected. This will enable you to render and interpret images and materials as part of your own logical progression or journey.

9–10 Juxtaposition
The images on the left-hand side of these sketchbook pages inspired the details on the facing pages.

Mood-, theme- and storyboards

Mood-, theme- and storyboards are made up as collages and, as the name suggests, are generally mounted on board, which makes them more durable. Mood-, theme- and storyboards are essentially a distillation of your research. In a sense, they are the 'presentation' version of the research book. Not all of the research that you have done will be useful when you are designing and so a mood-, theme- or storyboard can be helpful to show clearly the themes, concepts, colours and fabrics that will be used to design the season's collection. Keywords, such as 'comfort' or 'seduction', might also be included to communicate the story or convey a feeling. If the collection must be tailored to a particular client, the images may be more specifically attuned to the perceived lifestyle/ identity of the potential client.

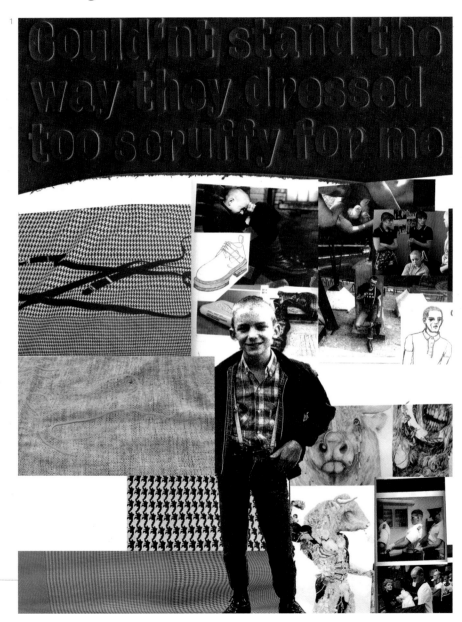

1 **Moodboard**

Example of a moodboard showing fabrics, details and research images.

< The research book
Mood-, theme- and storyboards
In fashion: Louise Gray >

2

2–3 Moodboard
The top moodboard
shows fabrics,
photographs and
ideas for designs.
The moodboard
below shows research
images, fabrics, colours
and design ideas.

3

In fashion:
Louise Gray

What role does research play in your design practice? Do you enjoy doing research?

Research is completely imperative, important and something that I have learned to collect and do constantly.

What inspires you?

Life; I'm drawn to energy and fun, and love, and obsessive things.

What is your approach to research? Is it an organic process of gathering references or do you have an idea for a theme and gather research accordingly?

I'm inspired by whatever I am into at the time; I become really absorbed by things, be it what I'm wearing, reading or listening to. I move on every season, but naturally I grow out of things and information, and move forward.

What do you actually do with your research while you are working with it?

I create a research wall – which also helps me link the information through to fabrics. I keep what I still like at the end: the rest I throw out.

At what point do you research fabric? And at what point in the design process do you begin to work on your fabric ideas?

From the beginning. It's something I think of, being textile-led; it's the basis of what I do.

Do you give yourself a deadline for the design?

I never cut off my mind – I can change or think and add things up until the last remaining few minutes of the process.

Is there a pattern to how you design?

Absolutely not, it's however I'm feeling each season.

Do you prefer to design in 2D, 3D or a combination of both?

I think you need both hand in hand.

How do you decide on which designs will actually make the collection and at what point do you stop designing a collection?

There are pieces that are certain from the beginning and others that are always a work in progress until the end.

Which part of creating a collection, from beginning to end, do you enjoy the most and why?

The research, the fabrics, fittings – seeing the reality of the clothing is fun.

1

1–4 **Autumn/Winter 2012**
Key looks from Louise Gray's Autumn/Winter 2012 collection.

Fashion file
Louise Gray was born in Fraserburgh, Scotland, and studied Textile Design at the Glasgow School of Art and at Central Saint Martins, London, where she completed her MA. Design collaborations include Cotton USA, Judy Blame, Nicholas Kirkwood, the Smiley Company and Crown Paint. Louise is also sponsored by the Centre for Fashion Enterprise.

5

5–6 **Louise Gray**
Key looks from Louise
Gray's Autumn/Winter
2012 collection featuring
a bold use of colour and
pattern.

Research exercises

From reading this chapter, you will have come to understand the importance of research for design. The most basic form of research for a fashion designer is the investigation into clothes, past and present. This is an ongoing activity and will hopefully be a fulfilling one as you learn more about clothing, fashion, its history and its potential. Research becomes more personal when developing a theme or concept for your own design work. It is important to be able to produce research that communicates to others the things that you are looking at, the 'story' of your work.

Exercise 1

You will find it extremely useful to create a personal collection of images of clothes that you like, are inspired by, or are just interested in for a particular detail. This collection of fashion references can take the form of a scrapbook or a file of images that you have collected over a period of time. It should be an ongoing activity. It will become a reference book and part of your own personal library that you will probably return to time after time, and it should become a personal source of inspiration for you. Hopefully, it will help to kick-start the design process at those times when you are simply not feeling inspired.

- Start to collect and compile a file or scrapbook of fashion and clothing references.

- A 'file' in this sense refers to a ring binder file. The advantage of using a file is that it will allow you to change the order of pages and add to them when you want or need to.

- If you prefer to start a scrapbook, then choose the size of your book carefully. A4 Letter (8.3 x 11.7 inches) may be too small as it will only allow one magazine tear sheet per page and your book will be more visually interesting if images are juxtaposed.

- Think about how you organize the images you have collected – you may decide to organize them into sections, for example, using headings such as 'Historical', 'Contemporary', or 'Details'.

Exercise 2

Take a day trip, or a journey around your local environment.

- Take with you a camera, drawing paper, pencils, some colour art materials (such as coloured pencils), an eraser and a pencil sharpener.

- Forget what you know about the environment; try to see it with fresh eyes and think about what you see as a potential source of theme for your design work – it could be the local architecture or the natural landscape. It might be a museum of objects or an art exhibition.

- The theme should be broad enough that it includes references to form, structure, pattern, line, colour and texture. However, it is important that you don't worry about how you will design from your theme just yet; this will inhibit your choice of theme, and the exciting thing about design is working when there are no preconceived outcomes.

- Record what you see with photographs, drawings, postcards and any relevant found objects. Try to accurately capture the colours that you see.

- When you have returned from your trip, review the research that you have gathered; lay it out in front of you and consider whether you have enough. It might be useful to back up this 'primary' research (research gathered first-hand from real sources) with some 'secondary' research (sourced images that are reproductions – for example, any images from the Internet). Think about other possible sources of research you could explore, for example, from a library or bookshop, or from an online search.

- Review your images – do any of them make you think of certain fabric or textures? If you have access to fabric shops, go and gather some fabric swatches to augment your research. There may be other sources of fabric available to you, such as markets or second-hand clothing stores (you could cut up existing clothes!).

- Look for some fashion references that relate to your theme or that you might want to incorporate within it. The strong horizontal, vertical or diagonal lines of modern architecture might be echoed in the seam lines on a dress or the shape of a building might be similar to its silhouette. Be considered about the references that you choose and make sure that there is a clear link to your other research.

Exercise 3

Choose what format your sketchbook will take and begin to compile your research. Your research book should be like a 'story' of your theme. Think about how your theme communicates on the pages; does it tell a story and would somebody understand the essence of your theme if they were to look through the book without you being there? You can write the story in it but no one wants to read an essay!

- Putting together your research book should be an organic process – try not to leave too many gaps that you 'will go back to and fill in later' because chances are that you won't! Also, you will learn from 'doing', so it is better to complete a page and then move on.

- Remember to consider the composition across the double page – even though there is a fold down the centre of the page it is in fact one whole page, so think about working across it.

- Your research book should include the following things:

  1) collage

  2) drawing (use a viewfinder to isolate parts of an image and draw what you see)

  3) juxtaposition (where you are making a connection between the things that you have gathered).

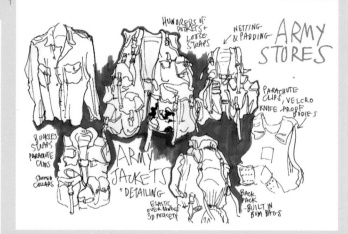

1 Drawings of garments from an army surplus shop.
2 Photographs of the City of London.
3 Fashion references.
4 Fabrics.

In context:
Alexander McQueen

In this chapter, we have looked at the fundamental role that research plays in the design process, how to begin your research and how to source, manipulate and format it.

Many designers use research creatively, to give themes and context to the clothes that they design. This not only enables them to focus their thinking behind their collections, but also adds a 'story' that is useful to communicate the designs.

Alexander McQueen's collections, which he first showed in 1992, each had a strong sense of narrative that could not have happened without the research and development of a theme. The subjects for the collections informed not only the clothes but also their presentation on the catwalk. In fact, according to Sarah Burton, his assistant who took over creative direction of his label after his death in 2010, McQueen would apparently sometimes conceive the catwalk presentation before he had even designed the clothes.

McQueen employed several key themes throughout his career: natural history, films, world costume and culture, and muses. He seldom made an entire collection around natural history but often included motifs such as birds' wings, feathers and shells as details in his garments. Isabella Blow said that the silhouette and cut of his clothes reminded her of birds.

1

1   **La Dame Bleue**
Dress from Spring/
Summer 2008. McQueen
was frequently inspired
by birds.

2

2 Widows of Culloden
Lace evening dress with
antler headdress from
Autumn/Winter 2006.

▶ In context: Alexander McQueen

3 The Dance of the Twisted Bull
Tailored outfit inspired by Spanish matadors for Spring/Summer 2002.

The films directed by Alfred Hitchcock often inspired McQueen, who even went so far as to name his collections after the movies (for example, 'The Birds' (Spring/Summer 1995) and 'The Man Who Knew Too Much' (Autumn/Winter 2005)). He would weave the story of the clothes loosely around the screenplays; the clothes were not literal interpretations of the film's costumes, but they might include references to fabric, cut, detail and mood. For 'The Man Who Knew Too Much', the clothes had an identifiably 1950s cut.

For a ready-to-wear collection for the Paris house Givenchy (Autumn/Winter 1999–2000), McQueen was inspired by Ridley Scott's seminal film 'Blade Runner', in particular the 'replicant' character Rachael (played in the film by Sean Young). There were direct references to the characters' costumes in the tailored collection and in the styling of the models. Some were even smoking on the catwalk as did Rachael in the film.

McQueen was inspired by both real and imagined women who became muses for his work. Perhaps the most poignant occasion was his 'La Dame Bleue' collection (Spring/Summer 2008), created in homage to his close friend and champion, the late magazine editor, Isabella Blow. Many of the models wore hats created by Philip Treacy: Isabella Blow was famous as a hat wearer and, fittingly, Philip Treacy, like McQueen himself, was one of her discoveries.

For 'The Dance of the Twisted Bull' (Spring 2002), McQueen referred to Spanish culture. Matadors' costumes inspired the cropped and sharply tailored jackets and slim trousers. One model wore a mutated red flamenco dress, pierced by two spears – a visual reference to bullfighting.

McQueen often referred to his own Scottish heritage. An early collection called 'Highland Rape' (Autumn/Winter 1995–96) was inspired by the eighteenth-century Jacobite Risings and the nineteenth-century Highland Clearances, both highly charged emotional and political events in Scottish history, which McQueen combined with inferences to contemporary sexual politics in his collection. For Autumn/Winter 2006–07, McQueen presented a sequel called 'Widows Of Culloden', a tribute to the women who lost their husbands in the bloody battle of Culloden, the final confrontation of the Jacobite Rising in 1746.

Muses

In order to create a narrative in their work, a designer might seek inspiration from a muse. According to Greek mythology, the muses were goddesses who inspired the creation of literature and the arts. In fashion design, a muse can be a real or imagined person, a fantasy or an idealized archetype. Maybe she is a friend of or collaborator with the designer whose style inspires them. The designer will hold an image of this person in mind when designing. The muse might be the designer's ideal customer or an ambassador for his or her style.

The Italian aristocrat Marchesa Luisa Casati (1881–1957) was often regarded as a muse to many artists and designers of her own time, and latterly to designers of our own era, including John Galliano and Alexander McQueen ('Sarabande', Spring/Summer 2007), due to her striking, unconventional looks and extravagant and eccentric life.

4

4 **Sarabande**
Spring/Summer 2007
sheer evening dress with
boned shoulders and
distressed flowers.

2 Design

Once your research has been collated, you can start on the design. But there is nothing more intimidating than a blank page. The process can be very frustrating; even when the designs start to come together, it can take a while before any of them are very satisfactory. This is a natural part of the design process. Many early designs are thrown away – and you might even begin to question your abilities. Don't panic! It takes time to hit your stride, and after sweating a while over the page, better ideas will start to emerge. Explore every possibility that comes to mind and discard nothing at this stage. You might discover the potential of an idea later on when you look back over your designs.

Design identity

A garment design needs three basic ingredients:

1) silhouette, proportion and line

2) detail

3) fabric, colour and texture.

Silhouette, proportion and line refer to the basic shape of the garment or outfit; its overall shape or how the body is broken up. Details give the garment focus and finish. Clothes are obviously made in fabric, and all fabric has colour and texture.

A designer's identity or style comes with time; but the clothes themselves also need an identity, or to form part of a vision, in order to stand apart from the competition. For example, while Chanel's identity is far-reaching and stays on track over many seasons, the identity of a collection of clothes may be based on the use of silhouette, proportion and line, detail or fabric for a single season.

Certain elements should run through the designs to give them coherence. It could be where an armhole is cut, the placement of a seam on the body in a particular way, or a method of finishing the fabric. If these elements tie in strongly with your theme to work as a 'whole', you are on your way to making a real statement with your designs.

1–2 **A coherent collection**

These design drawings are all from the same collection. Silhouettes, details and fabrics are repeated throughout to give the collection coherence.

'Fashion is very important.
It is life-enhancing and, like
everything that gives pleasure,
it is worth doing well.'

Vivienne Westwood

Ideal bodies

Historically, fashionable clothing was designed to enhance and idealize the natural silhouette of the human form by exaggerating certain parts of the body to create an 'hourglass' silhouette. The 'ideal' body shape continues to be based on an 'hourglass' today; however, most clothes follow the line of the body itself and the fashionable silhouette is less enhanced than it was before. This is partly because it is easier than ever to forego aids such as the corset or bustle and to alter the body itself by living a healthy lifestyle or making use of cosmetic surgery. But the evolution of the silhouette also relates to changing social and cultural trends.

Nip and tuck

The corset, as we know it, has been worn by women – and men – since the early part of the sixteenth century. Since that time, various contraptions have been added to corsets to exaggerate the hips and buttocks in different ways. Petticoats, farthingales, panniers, crinolines and bustles are all devices that have been fashionable at different times in the last 500 years and used to accentuate the shapeliness of the human body, as well as to project a shifting ideal of the female and male forms.

1 **Hourglass silhouette**
These examples show off typical idealized Victorian hourglass figures.

2 **Corsets and bustles**
Examples of corsets and hooped skirts with bustles that are designed to exaggerate the buttocks.

2

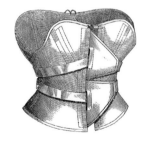

Changing shapes

Dior's 'New Look' collection of 1947 was created in response to the sparing use of fabrics that occurred as a result of rationing during the war years and involved a conscious feminization of the female form. It was defined by the generous use of luxurious fabrics and an accentuated wasp-waisted silhouette with widely flared skirts over padded hips, and its influence endured throughout the 1950s.

Corsets have also affected the shape of the chest, from the cleavage of the eighteenth and nineteenth centuries through to the mono-bosom of the early twentieth century. The supported chest reached a climax with the torpedo-like girdles and bras of the late 1940s and 1950s, revived and refigured in Jean Paul Gaultier's signature bra tops of the early 1990s.

4

3

3 1950s
A Christian Dior day dress from 1955 displaying the silhouette Dior first developed with his 'New Look' collection; sloping shoulders, a narrow waist and a full skirt.

4 1960s
The model Jean Shrimpton in a typical 1960s dress by Mary Quant.

5

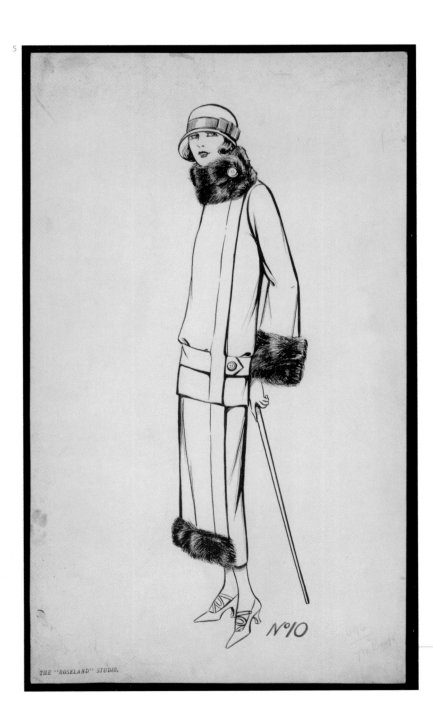

THE "ROSELAND" STUDIO.

In the 1920s and later in the 1960s, fashionable women adopted a radical silhouette that subverted the hourglass form. The 1920s silhouette was less constrained than what had preceded it – although, perversely, curvier women were required to artificially flatten their bodies with tube-like bandeaux in order to fit with the times. The 1960s silhouette went hand-in-hand with the trend for a more boyish look. Fashionable women wore their hair short, and, if they were lucky, already had flat chests, narrow shoulders and hips, which naturally complemented miniskirts and dresses.

Another example of an enhanced silhouette that was hugely popular in the 1980s and 1990s, as well as more recently in the late 2000s, was the use of exaggerated shoulder pads in what became known in the 1990s as 'power dressing'. The exaggerated shape became synonymous with strength, authority and the excesses of capitalism. The large pads allowed unstructured garments to hang from them, but as garments became more fitted the triangulation became more extreme. Giorgio Armani was a designer heavily associated with this look.

More recently, we have seen the return of the 'power shoulder' made fashionable by its use in collections by Christophe Decarnin for French fashion house Balmain (see page 18). The key use of the strong-shouldered silhouette was here combined with a more body-conscious form, often worn with skinny trousers or jeans.

5 **1920s**
A fashion illustration from the 1920s showing a typical straight up-and-down silhouette from the time.

Silhouette

Our first impression of an outfit when it emerges on the catwalk is created by its silhouette, which means that we look at its overall shape before we interrogate the detail, fabric or texture of the garment.

Silhouette is a fundamental consideration in your decision making. Which parts of the body do you want to emphasize and why? A full skirt will draw attention to the waist, forming an arrow shape between waist and hem. Wide shoulders produce the same result and can also make the hips look narrower. The waist itself does not have to be fixed as it is anatomically placed. It can be displaced through curved side seams or the raising or lowering of a horizontal (waist) line. The silhouette can also be affected by using fabric to create volume around the body or by making it close-fitting to accentuate it.

Choosing the size of a shoulder pad or where the waist is to be accentuated may seem like small decisions to make, but these subtle choices about silhouette give your clothes a unifying identity and stop them from becoming generic shapes. For example, Alexander McQueen's early collections in the 1990s suggested strong female sexuality and power through severe, close-fitted tailoring and shoulder pads that formed right angles to the neck. At a time when other designers were avoiding excessive shoulder pads because of their connotations with the 1980s and early 1990s, McQueen's shoulder line was aggressive and bold.

1

1 **Viktor & Rolf**
'No' Pantsuit by Viktor & Rolf for the Summer 1999 'Backlight' collection.

2

2 **Rick Owens**
This jacket by Rick Owens
for the Autumn/Winter
2011 collection uses
shoulder pads to create
an exaggerated curved
shoulder line, which
strongly reinforces the
silhouette.

3

The sculptural silhouette

Choosing the subtleties of silhouette and cut is essential, but some designers choose to make bolder statements by working far more sculpturally on the body. Leigh Bowery was an Australian designer and performance artist who died in 1994. He appeared to be completely unconcerned with convention or perceptions of taste, possibly because he never trained formally in fashion design. Bowery constantly experimented with his own silhouette, augmenting and constricting it, using boning, padding and even gaffer tape. He even displaced his own flesh (hence the gaffer tape) so that the line between (temporary) body modification and clothing became blurred. Leigh explained: 'Because I'm chubby, I can pleat the flesh across my chest and hold it in place with heavy-grade gaffer tape. Then, by wearing a specially constructed, under-padded bra, I create the impression of a heaving bosom with a six-inch cleavage.'

The clothes would often fit because he altered the shape of his own body. Bowery's body was capable of innumerable shapes and forms. 'The idea of transforming oneself gives courage and vigour. It reduces the absurdity; you can do anything dressed like this. I want to disturb, entertain and stimulate. It's more about silhouette alteration than restriction, though I do like that frisson of sexual danger. I like to think that I reform rather than deform the body,' he went on to explain.

(*Leigh Bowery: The Life and Times of an Icon*, Sue Tilley)

4

3–4 **Leigh Bowery**
Australian performance
artist, fashion designer
and icon, Leigh Bowery.

Parodying the silhouette

For the Comme des Garçons Spring/Summer 1997 collection, down pads were sewn into dresses in irregular places, creating a new silhouette and challenging preconceptions of the body and conventions of beauty by making the wearer look ill-proportioned and deformed.

Dutch designers Viktor & Rolf also explore the sculptural potential of silhouette. Their clothes often parody recognizable forms, historical references and traditional haute couture, but with fresh vision and humour. Scale and volume are taken to extremes, and in so doing they display their mastery over construction and tailoring and an understanding of the symbolic value of clothing.

5

5 **Comme des Garçons**
Dress by Comme des Garçons for their Spring/ Summer 1997 collection featuring down pads.

6
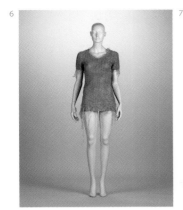

7

8

9

10

11

12

13

14

6–14 **Viktor & Rolf**

Viktor & Rolf, Haute Couture Autumn/Winter 1999–2000 collection, First, Second, Third, Fourth, Fifth, Sixth, Seventh, Eighth and Final Preparation. This series of nine outfits by Dutch designers Viktor & Rolf was inspired in part by Russian matryoshka dolls. The smallest outfit was shown on a model and then the next outfit was fitted over the top. This continued until the model was wearing nine outfits, one on top of the other, with each garment augmenting the silhouette of the previous outfit.

Proportion and line

The proportions of a garment develop from the silhouette. If the silhouette is the overall shape of the garment, then proportion is how the body is divided up either through lines (horizontal, vertical, diagonal or curved) or with blocks of colour or fabric. Every time we shop for clothes or get dressed we are playing with the perceptions of our own proportions. How and where we break up our bodies with horizontal hemlines, trouser widths, necklines and the position and emphasis of the waist depends on what flatters us.

The line of the garment generally refers to its cut; where seams and darts are placed on the body and the effect that they have visually. Confusingly, some designers will refer to the line of a garment when they actually mean its silhouette. The important thing to remember about any lines that are created on clothes is that they must be judged visually and balanced against each other as well as against any other nearby details – for example, openings, necklines and pockets.

1 **Celine**
The top in this outfit by Celine for their Autumn/ Winter 2011 collection uses a stark panel of black to slim the body; the proportion of black to white makes the shoulders appear narrower.

2 **Stella McCartney**
The black bustier and peplum of this top from McCartney's Autumn/ Winter 2011 collection creates the illusion that the waist is smaller than it actually is, whilst giving the body a more curvaceous appearance. Bringing the side seams forward in this manner has a flattering effect on the body.

< Silhouette
Proportion and line
God is in the details >

3

General rules of proportion and line

Vertical lines lengthen the body

Horizontal lines emphasize width

Straight lines are perceived to be hard and masculine

Curved lines are considered to be soft and feminine

Seams and darts are not standard and can be moved around the body

Garments can be of any length, creating horizontal lines across the body

Layers of clothing create multiple lines

3 **Prada**

The use of contrasting patterns on this Prada dress from Spring/Summer 2011 has the potential to make the wearer appear slimmer. The baroque pattern on the sides and the middle of the dress also lessen the impact of the horizontal stripes which can widen the body.

God is in the details

An outfit can have a dramatic silhouette and good line, but without great detailing it can appear amateur and unresolved. Outfits that lack detail can survive on the catwalk, but will not bear close scrutiny – for example, on the rail in a shop. Details in clothes are often the clincher when it comes to persuading someone to part with their money. Detailing is particularly important in menswear, where outlandish silhouette, line, fabric and pattern are generally off-putting to what is a largely conservative clientele.

Details are practical considerations: which fastening to choose, which type of pocket to have and how much top-stitching to use. Clever use of detail can also be used to give a collection of clothes a unique identity or signature; cutting a pocket in a particular way, using an embellishment in one area of a garment or the finishing of an edge can help to differentiate the garments of one designer from those of another.

Thinking about pocket types and fastenings might seem a little mundane, but choosing these things doesn't have to be like shopping for items from a catalogue. Although a pocket, for example, has a generic function and the concept is fixed, it doesn't mean that it needs to be conceived in a formulaic way. There are rules about how certain pockets are made and how these should look, but these notions can (and should) be distorted and reinvented. Fashion rules are made to be broken, after all.

1 **Magician Coat**
Designed by Boudicca for the Autumn/Winter 2005 collection. The front has a 'fake' revere collar (a flat, V-shaped collar) that is seamed in. The cuffs are 'striped' with top-stitching, as are the small circular panels on the shoulders. The line of the fringed circle gives the effect of epaulettes.

< Proportion and line
God is in the details
Fabric, colour and texture >

2

2 **Explode and Simulation**
'Explode Pocket' shirt
and 'Pocket One' jacket,
Spring/Summer 2005,
and Simulation skirt,
Autumn/Winter 2005, all
by Boudicca. Both shirt
and jacket have suspended
pockets. The shirt has an
'exploding' collar and the
jacket has multiple vents at
the back of the sleeves.

Fabric, colour and texture

You must understand the different varieties and qualities of fabric before you can apply them to a design. If the fabric is already in front of you, then knowing what you can design with it is paramount. For example, chiffon won't make a tailored jacket as well as will a wool fabric, and leather will not drape as well as will a fabric cut on the bias (across the grain).

Fabric choices are often dictated by your theme and season. Your theme may suggest a mood or colour palette that can then be interpreted into fabric. The season that you are designing for directs the weights, and to a degree, the textures that you will work with. Lighter fabrics tend to be used more in Spring/Summer collections and heavier fabrics, suitable for outerwear, tend to be used more for Autumn/Winter. Season can also influence colour. Lighter colours are often used more in Spring/Summer as are darker tones in Autumn/Winter, but this is not a firm rule. The feel and drape of a fabric will guide you as to what type of garment you can make with it – and this familiarity will buy you experience.

The way in which you choose to adopt colour is generally an issue of personal taste and there are few rules, although some colour combinations should generally be avoided. Red and black together can look clichéd (though McQueen would often put the two together masterfully). Traditionally, black and navy would not be worn together, but this is no longer a hard-and-fast rule. Too many primary colours can look garish or cheap, though in the right hands it can work, often by complementing them with a more subdued colour. Some colours don't work well next to certain skin tones. Beige and other 'flesh' tones can make skin look pink or red. Using a small amount of a colour as a highlight or accent when contrasted with other colours can have a stronger impact than by using large blocks of competing colour.

1

1 **Marc Jacobs**
The use of rubber for fashion is not uncommon, but here Marc Jacobs covers a dress in rubber sequins in a subtle colour to create an effect like fish scales for his Autumn/Winter 2011 collection.

< God is in the details
Fabric, colour and texture
Rendering your ideas >

2

2 Prada

Prada often combines fabrics, colours and textures to innovative effect. This dress from Autumn/Winter 2011 combines fur, large transparent sequins, blue socks and snakeskin.

'I try to draw from day to day. Things I find and things I see…. I'm trying to define a style that has nothing to do with fashion; it's more about individuality.'

Alexander McQueen

3

Colours and seasons

Each season tends to highlight specific fashionable colours. Trend forecasters predict which colours will be prevalent by analysing catwalk shows and creating an overview of that season's most popular colours. Some colours are enduring, however. Black tends to be constantly in fashion as it is slimming and can easily be worn with other colours. Certain colour palettes become synonymous with certain designers. For example, Rick Owens and Ann Demeulemeester typically use blacks, greys, muted colours and neutrals. Designers also make use of certain patterns as part of their signature. Paul Smith has become associated with a certain candy-stripe pattern and Missoni is known for its knitted zigzag.

You should endeavour to develop a range of colours and fabrics when designing. Any initial colour and fabric choices might need building on to fill in gaps. For example, a choice of five colours or fabrics may need an additional two to make the palette flow. Initial fabric choices may not have the breadth of weights and textures necessary to design a variety of clothing.

3 **Jil Sander**
This Jil Sander outfit by Raf Simons for Spring/ Summer 2011 uses blocks of strong colour teamed with black trousers, which help to temper the brightness of the top half of the outfit.

'Some people focus on retro, meaning sixties and seventies revivals. Some people stick to very traditional classic clothing, what we call "real" clothes, very easy to put on, simple clothes. I wanted to create something that didn't belong to any of those categories, and go forward.'

Rei Kawakubo

< God is in the details
Fabric, colour and texture
Rendering your ideas >

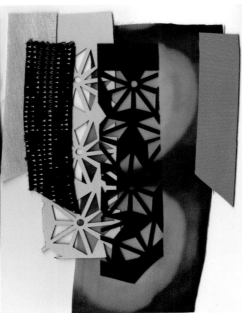

● 4–6 **Fabrics**
These are initial ranges of fabrics that have been gathered in sketchbooks. Each range explores a variety of fabrics, colours and textures.

4

5

6

Rendering your ideas

Drawing is a tool with which to communicate your design ideas – and is a means of literally getting what's in your head down onto paper. Ideas can be worked out three-dimensionally on the mannequin, but even this method of designing requires development on paper at some stage. It is not essential to be great at drawing to be a good designer, but it helps.

Drawing can be an intimidating activity, especially if you're out of practice. The thing to remember is that unless you plan on being a fashion illustrator, it is the design that is most important, not the drawing. Practice and repetition are key to improving drawing skills, though repetition itself should be thoroughly interrogated.

A bad habit or mannerism can become automatic if you are not actively thinking about what is being rendered; a claw shape where the hand should be becomes less hand-like the more you lose your objectivity.

As a designer working primarily with the body, it will be useful for you to undertake some life-drawing classes at some stage. Drawing the naked human body will help you to understand anatomy, musculature and proportion, as well as how the body works in terms of balance and stance. Drawing a dressed form is useful too, in order to understand how clothes work on the body. Both exercises require you to use art media and to experiment with mark making (how art materials are used to put ideas down on paper).

Fashion illustration

It is useful to make a distinction between fashion drawing and fashion illustration. A fashion illustration is not so much about the design, but about capturing the spirit of the clothes. Illustration can be used to express a mood or to give the clothes context by setting a scene in which the clothes might be worn, or by representing the kind of person who might wear the clothes through styling, make-up, hair and pose. A fashion illustration does not need to show the whole of a garment unless it is used in a portfolio in which a design has not been made up into a real outfit or garment; here, the illustration takes the place of a photograph, showing how the garment would look on the body.

1 **Illustration**
This final illustration started as a hand drawing before being scanned and enhanced using image-editing software.

< Fabric, colour and texture
Rendering your ideas
In fashion: Richard Gray >

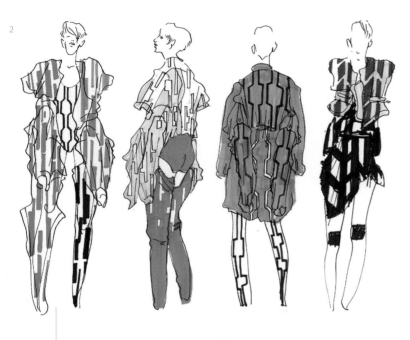

2

Fashion drawing

A fashion drawing is about communicating your design ideas, although it can also be about capturing the spirit of the clothes. A fashion drawing is a figurative form that is used to get ideas down quickly. It doesn't need to be fancy or the best drawing that you have ever done. What it does need to be is fairly proportional; it has to bear a convincing resemblance to a 'real' human form. If the proportions of your drawing are too abnormal, this will follow through to the proportions of your designs; what looks good on a figure that has too-long legs won't necessarily look good on a real person.

A fashion drawing also needs to be a fairly fast drawing; in an ideal world, when the creative juices are flowing, ideas come to you rapidly and need to be put down on paper quickly before they are forgotten. And forgotten they will be, because the mind has a habit of moving on to other ideas. As you draw your designs, try to put down as much relevant information as possible; your designs are not only about silhouette and detail – they're about colour and fabric, too.

But fashion drawing and illustration are not solely about rendering the human form in a realistic manner. Some fashion drawings are so stylized that they seem to rely little on a real human figure; they rather rely on a knowledge of fashion drawing itself (in other words, they reference other fashion drawings) and some fashion drawings become more like cartoons. With practice, your fashion drawing will eventually take on a character of its own and become as individual as your signature.

2 **Fashion drawing**
These quick and confident fashion drawings are made using marker pens.

3 **Mixed media**
Examples of John-Gabriel Harrison's design process where he has drawn over photographs of his toiles.

3

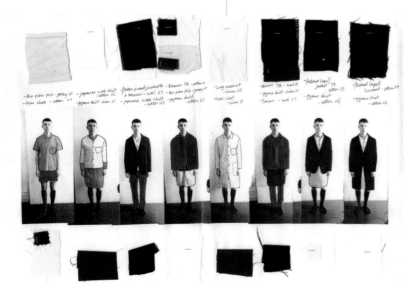

Templates

Design drawing is about speed; getting your ideas onto paper as quickly as possible before you forget them. If you are a beginner, you can use templates of pre-drawn figures that can then be traced through layout paper (or any other transparent paper), thereby speeding up the process of designing. Templates can be found in 'how to do fashion illustration/drawing' type books or can be developed from your own drawings. It is preferable to develop templates from your own drawings to keep them individual. But be warned: if you rely too much on templates it will mean that your freehand fashion drawing will suffer through lack of practice.

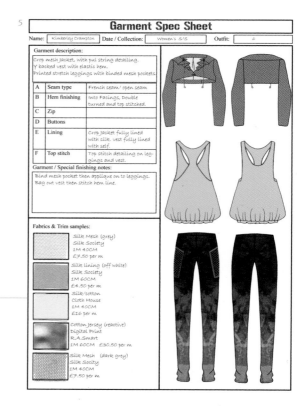

5

Garment Spec Sheet

Name: Kimberley Crampton   Date / Collection: Women's S/S   Outfit: 6

Garment description:
Crop mesh jacket, with pul string detailing.
'Y' backed vest with elastic hem.
Printed stretch leggings with binded mesh pockets

A	Seam type	French seam/ open seam
B	Hem finishing	Into Facings, Double turned and top stitched.
C	Zip	
D	Buttons	
E	Lining	Crop jacket fully lined with silk. vest fully lined with self.
F	Top stitch	Top stitch detailing on leggings and vest.

Garment / Special finishing notes:
Bind mesh pocket then applique on to leggings.
Bag out vest then stitch hem line.

Fabrics & Trim samples:

Silk Mesh (grey)
Silk Society
1M 400CM
£7.50 per m

Silk lining (off white)
Silk Society
1M 600CM
£4.50 per m

Silk/cotton
Cloth House
1M 400CM
£16 per m

Cotton Jersey (reactive)
Digital Print
R.A.Smart
1M 600CM £30.50 per m

Silk Mesh (dark grey)
Silk Soity
1M 400CM
£7.50 per m

4 **A 'line up'**
This is a drawing of a collection 'line up', where all the outfits are presented literally in a line so that they can be seen together as a coherent whole. Templates have been used to create these drawings.

5 **Garment spec sheet**
A spec sheet contains all the information that a manufacturer would require to actually make the garment.

4

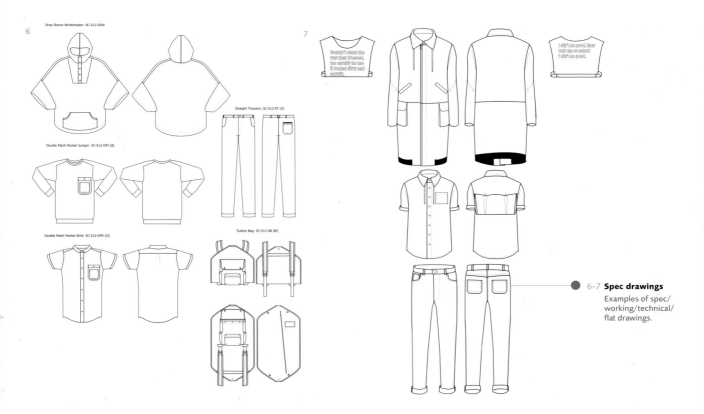

6   Drop Sleeve Windcheater: SC-S12-DSW

Double Patch Pocket Jumper: SC-S12-DPJ (B)

Double Patch Pocket Shirt: SC-S12-DPS (O)

Straight Trousers: SC-S12-ST (S)

'Sutton Bag: SC-S12-SB (BI)

7

6–7 Spec drawings
Examples of spec/working/technical/flat drawings.

Spec/working/technical/flat drawings

When drawing designs, you might include little artistic flourishes that have little to do with the design, but are more to do with mark making or how you imagine the fabric to fold and move. You may also have unresolved issues, such as fastenings, top-stitching, seams, darts, and so on, and these issues need to be addressed at some point. This can take place during pattern cutting and making the toile, but if someone else is going to cut the pattern for the garment these issues need to be addressed sooner rather than later.

Spec drawings (short for specification drawings, but also sometimes called working drawings, technical drawings, or 'flats') are flat drawings of the garment, front and back, as if the garment is laid out on a table, showing all its details and accurate proportions.

Spec drawings are line drawings only; they are purely about structure and detail. Many are executed with a black fine-line pen. One pen (for example, 0.8mm width) may be used for outline, seams, darts and details (depending on what they are) and a finer pen (for example, 0.3mm width) can be used for top-stitching.

There are two methods of representing top-stitching: as a continuous fine line, which in fact it is; or more commonly as a dotted or dashed line. If using the latter method, make sure that the dots or dashes are neat, regular and dense or it may give the appearance of large, crude, hand-tacking stitches.

You might also choose a fine line for buttons, press-studs or other details; there is no single rule; as long as you communicate the garment accurately there should not be any problem.

In industry, the drawings are given to a pattern cutter so that he or she can cut the pattern for the design. The drawings should communicate the design accurately so that the pattern cutter doesn't have to second-guess any aspect of it, so the designs must be well thought through. Spec drawings are also useful for the sample machinist and help with construction when there is no toile available.

Spec drawing is one of the most important tools in design and so this needs to be practised until they are of a high standard! It is useful to learn how to do spec drawings freehand, but you can also learn to create them by using computer programs such as Adobe Illustrator.

In fashion:
Richard Gray

Please describe your job

I am commissioned to create fashion illustrations according to the client's creative brief. The client can vary, from editorial – magazines and books – to a couture, prêt-à-porter or high-street designer. I am expected to create a rough/line illustration initially, to showcase my ideas and in response to what I have been asked to do. If everyone involved is happy with this, I will then complete the finished artwork, all within a set time and deadline.

What was your career path to your current job?

I studied Fashion Design at Middlesex University, UK. During this time, I was entered for an illustration competition in Italy celebrating the great fashion illustrator Antonio Lopez. I didn't win, but came fourth, and was invited to Milan to meet Anna Piaggi of 'Vogue Italia'. From this meeting, I was asked to create illustrations for her in 'Vogue Italia', and also for 'Vanity' magazine.

On graduating, these first commissions made it much easier to get other people to see my portfolio, and I pursued my interest in fashion illustration as a career from then on.

What do you do on an average day?

Each day can vary so much from the next, depending on the turnaround of deadlines and the amount of time between them. I could be researching ideas, creating initial concept sketches, or creating final artwork.

What are your normal working hours?

My average working day is between 12 and 15 hours, due to the turnaround of work for deadlines. It can, however, be much less than that and occasionally much more; it isn't uncommon to work right through the night to get work completed to deadline. The flipside of this is that you can also get several days off in a row if you are between commissions. The demands of the job mean that it is unlikely to ever be nine to five, Monday to Friday.

What are the essential qualities needed for your job?

Creativity, the ability to understand a client's creative brief and what they are trying to achieve from your work, and the limitations or expectations of work created towards specific markets. Discipline to make sure that work is done to deadline, even if it means late nights. The ability to sometimes think outside the brief and to make sure that your personality still comes through in your work – the reason why you have been approached in the first place.

What is the best bit about your job?

The best part is the unpredictability of the working year; the surprise and delight when designers or magazines you admire ask you to work with them, and the variation in commissions from one to the next. It helps that I haven't restricted my career to one single style, so there's a lot of variety in what I am asked to do.

And the worst?

It sometimes feels like there are not enough hours in the day, but apart from that there is nothing to complain about.

Any advice you would give to someone wanting to get a job in your area of fashion?

Illustration is a career that can be very fulfilling, but like all freelance careers there are no guarantees. Not all people will like what you do, as art and illustration is such a subjective form, so don't be put off if you find your work is not to everyone's taste. Always listen to constructive criticism and know when to ignore it. Most of all, as important as it is to be creative, it is important to be reliable. The client wants the work done with as little fuss as possible. Everyone is busy, multitasking, with a million problems to solve every day. If you make their life that little bit easier by completing your work for them to deadline, completely answering their creative brief, they are more likely to come back to you again.

1 **Richard Gray**
'Biker', 2010.

2

Fashion file

Richard Gray is a fashion illustrator whose clients include: Alexander McQueen, Givenchy, Agent Provocateur, Vivienne Westwood, Miguel Adrover, Julien Macdonald, Kylie Minogue and William Baker, Boudicca, Oasis and Printemps. Editorially, he has worked for 'Vogue Pelle', Anna Piaggi's D.P. pages for 'Vogue Italia', 'V' magazine, 'Madame Figaro', 'Flaunt', 'The Observer Magazine', 'Vogue Gioiello', 'Los Angeles Times' magazine, 'Sleek', 'The Independent on Saturday Magazine', 'Mixte', 'Io Donna', 'JaLouse' (USA) and 'Entertainment Weekly', amongst many others.

2 **Richard Gray**
Boudicca Essays, 2010.

Portfolios

As a designer, your portfolio is one of the most important outcomes of all your hard work. The portfolio (also called a 'Book'), is how you collect your work in order to show it to others. Together with research sketchbooks, your portfolio is what you show to tutors, prospective investors or employers, stylists and journalists in order to pique their interest.

1

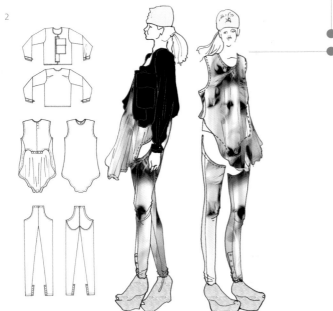

2

1–2 Student portfolios
Examples of work from student portfolios.

The graduate portfolio

The result of each assessment during and upon completion of a fashion degree course is generally a portfolio of work. Your graduation portfolio will include fashion drawings, fashion illustrations, working drawings, fabric swatches, moodboards, fabric boards, and photographs of actual garments and outfits. There might also be samples of details, including examples of embroidery or a particular method of finishing a garment.

An independent designer's portfolio

As an independent designer, your portfolio will eventually become much more about recording the clothes and the collections that you have made. There may be catwalk shots or the results of a shoot styled by you or with a stylist of your collection. The portfolio also becomes an archive of your press cuttings.

An industry portfolio

As a professional designer working for other companies, your portfolio will feature work that you have designed for your employers, including photos and sketches, as well as press images of your design work. Most of the design drawing that you do if you are working for a company will be executed as working drawings, so it is essential that you include evidence of this in the portfolio.

These last two examples of portfolios are very different in content and focus from the graduate portfolio. Whilst they represent a more professional body of work, this does not negate the importance of the graduate portfolio, which is the designer's first step towards a professional approach to a career in fashion design.

3

4

3–4 **Press portfolio**
Press cuttings from Richard Sorger's press portfolio.

In fashion:
Peter Jensen

Please describe your brand

We celebrated our ten-year anniversary in 2011. We sell to stores such as Dover Street Market in London, and Opening Ceremony which has stores worldwide.

How many collections or projects do you work on in a season?

At this point, it is around three collections.

What role does research have in your design practice? Do you enjoy doing research?

Yes I do like it a lot. It plays a big role in what we do here at Peter Jensen.

Fashion file

Originally hailing from Logstor, Denmark and now based in London, Peter Jensen has carved out a reputation as a designer whose impeccably produced creations thread together mischievous humour and a celebratory approach to individuality. Each collection references a famous woman whose style, spirit and attitude particularly appeals to the designer, from Sissy Spacek to Cindy Sherman.

What inspires you?

Every season we have a muse, always a woman. In the past, it has been women like Nancy Mitford and Sissy Spacek. For the Resort 2012 collection, it was Meryl Streep and the films 'Kramer vs. Kramer', 'The Deer Hunter' and 'Manhattan'. I always think of the women that we use for the collections as a working tool; it is a way for me to communicate with the stylist, photographer and the rest of the creative team that we work with. It becomes a story and sets up some rules to work within for me and the team.

What do you actually do with your research while you are working with it?

I work with it in a book – not a sketchbook, but an A3-size book (11.7 x 16.5 inches) that has been the same from the beginning. I like that because it makes it look uniform.

Which comes first – textiles or garment shapes?

I think that it's all a mix; sometimes it is the designs and sometimes it is the fabrics.

How do you approach the design – after the research is complete or during?

I always begin with the research. Having said that, I do like to work on the designs at the same time, just because you can see if you are going in the right direction and whether it looks okay or if you will need to start all over again.

Is there a pattern to how you design?

I prefer to draw at home and at the weekend. Every season, I start by watching the same Danish TV series, called 'Matador'. I must have seen it I don't know how many times, but it always puts me in a place of ease.

Do you prefer to design in 2D or 3D, or a combination of both?

2D; I think it suits the way that I draw and it's also the way that I was trained.

How do you decide on which designs will actually make the collection and at what point do you stop designing a collection?

We stop designing the day before the show – it is also at this point that the styles that aren't working get the death penalty. It all becomes clear what works and what doesn't once the stylist starts working on the show. Of course, we also have pieces that will make it into the sales collection but not into the show.

Which part of creating a collection, from beginning to end, do you enjoy the most and why?

I love to do the drawings, because it is at this point that you have the freedom to create something that is inside your head. I also like to do the fitting of the garments, because you can then see whether what you have been trying to say works, and whether the pattern cutter and other members of the team genuinely understand what you are trying to get across.

1–9 'Meryl', Resort 2012
Images from the Peter Jensen 'Meryl' Resort 2012 collection.

1

2

3

4

5

6

7

8

9

Design exercises

In this chapter, you have been introduced to some of the key elements that you will need to consider when you are designing. We have also discussed rendering your ideas. We have seen that your designs essentially need three basic ingredients in order to be successful:

1) silhouette, proportion, and line

2) detail

3) fabric, colour and texture.

Exercise 1

Develop a figure to use for your designs. This could be your own drawing or it might be developed from an existing template. If using an existing template, try to customize it in some way to make it more individual to you. Draw out a series of figures, either freehand or by using the template that you have developed. This will save time later and allow you to just 'dress' the figure, speeding up the design process. Try not to just draw one figure per page but instead draw a row of three–six figures depending on your page size and layout (are you working landscape or portrait?).

▪ Refer back to the research book you created for the exercises in Chapter 1. Look through the whole book and mark the pages with images that might inspire ideas for silhouette. Make a list if this helps. Don't just refer to the fashion images – think about how other images could inspire the form too; for example, a cathedral dome might inspire the shape of a skirt or the top of a sleeve. Make design drawings on your pre-drawn-out figures that focus on silhouette.

▪ Experiment with exaggerating different parts of the body; neck, shoulders, bust, waist, hips or legs. Ensure that these manipulations of silhouette also reference something directly from your research.

▪ Again, referring to your research, look for images that might inspire proportion and line. You could start by drawing lines on your figure, effectively 'cutting it up'. But try to take the lines that you draw directly from your research. Think about horizontal, vertical, diagonal, curved and angled lines.

▪ If you haven't already done so, do some additional research into details such as pockets, fastenings, embellishments and so on (then add this research to your fashion file). This is to make you aware of different details that you might not have noticed before; different collars, alternative ways of creating a pocket. Using your theme and your research book, design a series of pockets, collars, cuffs, openings, embellishments or other details. Draw these out on figures, placing the details where you intend them to go, or draw the details on their own.

Exercise 2

Using ideas generated in Exercise 1, combine ideas for silhouette, proportion and line, and detail into a new series of designs, so that each design has all of these ingredients. Try to generate as many ideas as possible.

▪ Practise and experiment using different types of coloured art materials that are available to you. When you are feeling more confident with their use, add colour to your existing designs. If you want to practise more before working on the original designs, then make black-and-white photocopies of the original drawings and work on these.

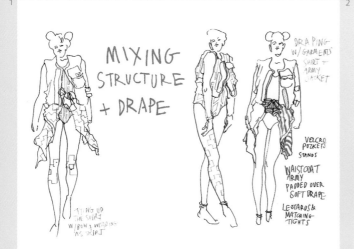

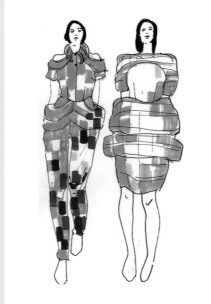
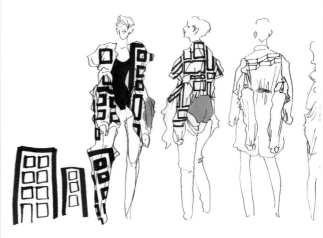

1 Details from army surplus are added to these designs.

2 A simplistic drawing of a building is used here to generate ideas for patterns.

3–5 Experiments with silhouette, proportion and line, detail and colour.

▶ **In context:**
Nicolas Ghesquière, Balenciaga

1

In this chapter, we have looked at how the design of clothes can be reduced to three fundamental 'ingredients': silhouette, proportion and line; detail; and fabric, colour and texture. These ingredients are employed by all designers, but in this case study we will look at Nicolas Ghesquière, creative director for Balenciaga since 1997, because each collection he designs explores new ideas and technologies, producing clothes that have no precedent. Every season therefore represents a complete surprise.

Nicolas Ghesquière is a rare creature; he appears to be a self-taught designer rather than one who followed the more conventional route of studying fashion at college or university. At the age of 15, he interned at Agnès B and then later for Jean Paul Gaultier. Afterwards, he worked as a freelance designer for Italian houses such as Trussardi and Callaghan, before joining Balenciaga to work on the licence diffusion line, the mass-produced output of the brand.

No two Balenciaga collections by Ghesquière are alike; he constantly innovates by using unexpected materials and techniques, and employing surprising changes of direction in his themes and cuts. But he is also respectful of the legacy of Cristóbal Balenciaga, often referring to the company archive in his designs and even reproducing classics from the archive for the label 'Balenciaga Edition'.

1 **Autumn/Winter 2008**
A simple dress made seductive with the use of a stiff, car-shiny fabric.

Cristóbal Balenciaga was known for his mastery of silhouette, which Ghesquière shares. For example, Ghesquière often features pronounced shoulders, either by introducing boxy cuts to the garments as seen in Spring/Summer 2012, or by using a variety of different techniques to create an exaggerated round shoulder, as in his Spring/Summer 2008 collection. In this collection there were common silhouettes, proportions and lines throughout and most of the outfits had exaggerated rounded shoulders and either a short skirt or skinny trousers. The same lines and details were repeated on many garments, such as the stitching detail used on the outside of the seams.

The designer has a refined eye for fabric and colour. Ghesquière often uses unconventional hi-tech fabrics like neoprene, latex and plastic to great effect, creating garments that look as though they have been moulded rather than cut in the traditional sense. Ghesquière treats colour graphically, enjoying metallic nail-polish shades accented with brighter tones or blocked in contrasting panels, like the jackets that started the catwalk show for Spring/Summer 2012.

Texture, too, is essential to the clothes. Whether using car-shiny latex, knitted leather, laser cutting, quilting or embellishing, the fabrics don't just feel modern – they feel almost futuristic!

2 **Autumn/Winter 2011**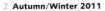
   The front of this jacket is
   made from knitted tubes
   of leather.

2

'It was interesting to explore historical clothes and to think about those textures, those embroideries, those materials and then to interpret them for a woman today, not as costume but as wardrobe.'

Nicolas Ghesquière at Balenciaga

▶ In context: Nicolas Ghesquière, Balenciaga

Ghesquière seeks out textile techniques that have seldom been seen in clothing before, or subverts and reinvents these for his own purposes. For example, knitted tubes of leather were used to create the front panels of jackets for Autumn/Winter 2011–12; whilst synthetic fabric was printed with text that was then laser-cut and manipulated into little quilted pods for Autumn/Winter 2010–11.

Most collections include one or more textile prints. For the Spring/Summer 2008 collection, the designer used a variety of intense florals bonded onto neoprene, a high performance sports fabric usually associated with wet suits. 'I'm exploring new territory, within the references of the house,' he said in an interview with the journalist Sarah Mower. The designs were varied and rarely used twice in the catwalk collection, but they all shared a common quality – an energetic and busy floral pattern. For the subsequent season, Ghesquière went in a completely different direction with prints that referred to Japanese art, incorporating images of Hokusai-like waves, sleeve tattoos and Japanese scenery.

Writing in the 'International Herald Tribune' in 2001, the critic Suzy Menkes enthused that Ghesquière represents 'the most intriguing and original designer of his generation. His collections are explorations of shape, volume and embellishment that seem totally new – yet reflect in a glancing abstract way the style of the iconic design house that shelters him: Balenciaga.'

3

3 **Autumn/Winter 2010–11**
The fabric of this top has been printed, then laser-cut and manipulated into little quilted pods.

4

4 Spring/Summer 2008
For this collection, Ghesquière used a variety of different prints, many floral, bonded to neoprene to give them a sculptural form. An exaggerated, rounded shoulder was common throughout.

Cristóbal Balenciaga

The House of Balenciaga was founded by the Spanish couturier Cristóbal Balenciaga in 1937 at Avenue George V in Paris, where it is still located today. The designer had previously worked for the legendary Christian Dior who may have influenced his mastery of silhouette. The company closed its doors in 1968; Cristóbal Balenciaga died in 1972. Balenciaga was relaunched in the 1980s and Nicolas Ghesquière eventually became creative director in 1997.

3 Fabrics and techniques

As a fashion designer, you will need to have an understanding of fabrics and what their properties are; for example, how fabrics are constructed, what they are made from and how they perform. This knowledge will then equip you to choose the right fabric for your designs.

It is also important to be aware of the various techniques that can be applied to your chosen fabric. This will give you endless possibilities in the creation of your designs; for example, a fabric could be dyed or printed to add extra colour, or be embellished, embroidered or pleated to give surface interest. Try to learn the names of as many fabrics and techniques as possible, as this will enable you to communicate your fabric ideas easily to others.

Lastly – and probably of most importance – the modern-day designer should consider the ethical impact that fabric has on the environment. When choosing a fabric, you should question whether the fibre is organic in origin, whether the dyes used to colour the yarn are eco-friendly or, for instance, whether the factory that the fabric is made in meets fair trade standards. Do you agree with using fur or leather? There are many ethical questions that you need to ask yourself and find the answers to.

Fabric

It is of fundamental importance for every designer to understand the unique properties and qualities of fabrics. Choosing the right fabric for a garment is crucial to its success.

Firstly, the weight and handle of a fabric will affect the silhouette of a garment, giving it shape and form or allowing it to drape; for example, silk will have more of a 'draping' quality than heavy wool, which will have more structure. When we talk about the 'handle' of a fabric, we are referring to how it feels in the hand, its texture and its weight, and also the way it hangs or drapes from the hand.

Secondly, a fabric will be chosen for its performance in relation to its function; for example, jeans must be comfortable, durable and long-lasting – and denim is the perfect fabric for this. A raincoat must ideally be lightweight, but still offer protection from the elements; a Teflon-coated cotton would be ideal for this kind of garment. A tight-fitting T-shirt would be best made in a stretchy, breathable fabric, possibly 100 per cent cotton-knitted jersey.

Finally, fabrics must be chosen for their aesthetic value; in other words, the way that they look and feel, as well as their colour, pattern or texture.

Let's look a little more closely at the defining characteristics of fabrics. What is the composition of a fabric? Are the fibres derived from natural or man-made sources? How is the fabric constructed? Is it knitted, woven or maybe crocheted, for example?

1

1–2 **Wonderland magazine**

Photoshoot by Elena Rendina for 'Wonderland' magazine (2011); these images show an exciting mix of colour, texture and pattern.

'Fashion is what one wears oneself.
What is unfashionable is what
other people wear.'

Oscar Wilde

2

Natural fibres

Natural fibres are derived from organic sources; these can be divided into plant sources (in other words, those composed of cellulose) or animal sources (those composed of protein).

Cellulose fibres

Cellulose is made of carbohydrate and forms the main part of plant cell walls. It can be extracted from a variety of plant forms to make fibres suitable for textile production. Here we are looking at fabrics that are most suitable for the production of garments; they must be soft enough to wear and not break up when worn or washed.

Cotton is a prime example of a plant fibre; it has a soft, 'fluffy' character and grows around the seed of the cotton plant; these fibres are harvested from the plant, then processed and spun into cotton thread. Cotton's enduring popularity lies in its extreme versatility; it can be woven or knitted into a variety of weights. It is durable and has breathable properties, which is useful in hot climates as it absorbs moisture and dries off easily.

Linen has similar properties to cotton, especially in the way that it handles, although it tends to crease more easily. It is produced from the flax plant and is commonly regarded as the most ancient fibre. Hemp, ramie and sisal are also used to produce fabrics as an alternative to cotton.

1

1 **Eppie Conrad**
Digitally printed cotton jersey by contemporary designer Eppie Conrad.

Organic fabric production

With most cotton production, farmers have used chemical fertilizers and pesticides on the soil and sprayed them on the plants in order to prevent disease, improve the soil and to increase their harvest. The chemicals are absorbed by the cotton plant and remain in the cotton during manufacture, which means that they still reside in the fabric that we end up wearing next to our skin. Due to the potential health hazards that this poses and the other environmental issues raised by such methods of cotton production, manufacturers are increasingly looking at ways to develop organic fibres that can be grown from non-genetically modified plants and processed without the use of artificial fertilizers and pesticides. Organic fabric production is a more expensive option, but it ultimately has a lower impact on the environment and is healthier for the consumer.

Katharine Hamnett and Edun were both pioneers in searching for organic solutions to fashion design in the 1980s; today, many fashion organizations choose to incorporate organically grown fabrics within their product ranges or to use fabrics which present an alternative to cotton.

2   **Kuyichi**
Organic fashion from Netherlands-based sustainable fashion company Kuyichi.

Protein fibres

Protein is essential to the structure and function of all living cells. Keratin comes from hair fibres and is the most commonly used protein fibre in textile production.

Sheep produce wool fleece on their skin for protection against the elements and this can be shorn at certain times of the year and spun into wool yarn. Different breeds of sheep produce different qualities of yarn. Wool has a warm, slightly elastic quality, but it doesn't react well to excessive temperatures; when washed in hot water it shrinks due to the shortening of fibres. Goats are also used to produce wool; certain breeds produce cashmere and angora. Alpaca, camel and rabbit are also used to produce fabrics with a warm, luxurious quality.

Silk is derived from a protein fibre and is harvested from the cocoon of the silkworm. The cocoon is made from a continuous thread that is produced by the silkworm as it wraps it around itself for protection. Cultivated silk is stronger and has a finer appearance than silk harvested in the wild. During the production of cultivated silk, the larvae is killed to enable the worker to collect the silk and unravel it as a continuous thread. In the wild, the silkworm chews its way out of its cocoon, thereby cutting into what would otherwise be a continuous thread.

Woollen fabrics

Fabrics made from wool tend to have warm and breathable characteristics. However, they can be rather unstable and when heat or friction is applied, they may be prone to shrinking. This is due to the fibres contracting.

4

3 **Sources of wool**
Natural fibres can originate from llamas, merino sheep and angora goats.

4 **Winni Lok angora mohair jumper**
Large floating yarns give a laddered effect to this jumper.

5 **Peter Jensen**
Double-layered lace and silk-effect dress by contemporary Danish designer Peter Jensen.

3

5

In fashion:
Virginia James, Poetry and Wrap

What is your job title?

My job title is creative and design director of Poetry and Wrap (selective marketplace).

What has your career path been so far?

I graduated from Kingston University back in 1983 following a foundation course in Art and Design at Manchester Polytechnic.

I worked on first graduating for Enrico Coveri in Florence, Italy for nine months. Then at Miss Selfridge (as their first in-house designer ever); Warehouse (head of design for four years); M&S (senior designer across blouses/knitwear/swimwear/tees/sportswear and dresses for six years); at Pringle (as head of design/creative head for two and a half years); at Whistles (as head of design for four years) and now at Poetry and Wrap!

So my career so far has nearly all involved womenswear.

Fashion file

Poetry was launched in 2005 and has an older customer base, featuring classic pieces with a laid-back look made from quality natural fabrics, such as merino wool, pure linen and silk. Poetry is an online and catalogue collection which followed the success of its sister company, Wrap.

What do you do on an average day?

Trend/fabric research, drawings/fittings, motivating the product developers and freelance designers, briefing the teams, sales analysis, shopping for ideas, and seeing/briefing colour and print designers.

How does Poetry differ from Wrap?

Poetry is simpler and more item-led for a slightly older customer.

Poetry seems to feature a lot of natural fibres: is this important to the brand?

Natural fibres are important to both brands – it's part of our ethos; we don't really like synthetics!

Where do you source your fabrics from?

We choose our fabrics based on previous seasons/my design brief. We see what the top name designers are doing and look for similar types. We work closely with our factories to develop our own fabrics from our brief; and we visit Première Vision/Texworld/London fairs and Pitti Filati.

How big a collection do you work on and how many collections do you create a year?

The collections should be around 60–80 pieces and we do two big ones and two mini ones a year.

How do you start to design a collection? Is research important? Where do you start?

I start with my own life, what I have been doing/looking at/visiting. I also gather info/pictures/samples from vintage fairs and travels. I then build my own brief and my world for the season.

How much of your work involves travelling for research or factory visits?

It's two thirds research and one third factory visits as this is really a product development role.

What kind of team do you work with?

We are really small; I am the only designer on Wrap with two developers and it's now the same on Poetry but I am building a small team with a few more people so that I can roll out the vision. There are only about 10 of us in total at the creative end.

The best and worst parts of your job?

I love my job. I hate it when the collection doesn't sell or the shoot goes wrong!

What advice would you give someone wanting a job in your area of fashion?

Keep working and be prepared to be involved in all areas even if you think it's junior. It's a small world and we all need to keep learning.

1 **Wrap**
Pieces from the Wrap Spring/Summer 2012 collection.

Man-made fibres

Man-made fibres are made from cellulosic and non-cellulosic fibres. Cellulose is extracted from plants, especially trees. Man-made fibres such as rayon, Tencel, acetate, triacetate and Lyocell are cellulosic fibres as they contain natural cellulose. All other man-made fibres are non-cellulosic, which means that they are made entirely from chemicals and are commonly known as synthetics.

Developments in the chemical industry in the twentieth century caused a transformation in fabric production. Chemicals that had previously been used for textile finishing techniques began to be used to extract fibres from natural sources in order to make new fibres.

Blended fabrics

Fabrics today are often formed of a blend of natural and man-made fibres. A fabric can thereby have the best properties of each fibre. For example, with a polyester/cotton mixed fabric, the cotton lends breathability and the polyester is crease-resistant and so easier to care for. With a cotton/lycra blend, the lycra will lend elasticity to the cotton fabric.

Rayon was one of the first man-made fabrics to be developed. It is extracted from cellulose and was developed to mimic the qualities of silk; to be strong, absorbent, to drape well and have a soft handle. Different chemicals and processes are used in the production of rayon, each with its own name; these include acetate rayon, cuprammonium rayon and viscose rayon, which is known commonly as viscose. Lyocell and modal are evolved from rayon.

Tencel was developed to be the first environmentally friendly man-made fabric. It is made from sustainable wood plantations and the solvent used to extract it can be recycled. It is a strong fabric that drapes like silk, with a soft handle.

1 **Fabrics made from man-made and synthetic fibres**

Top row: fabrics include cotton/nylon/lycra mix, nylon, nylon ripstop, poly-cotton, Teflon-coated poly-cotton, polyester/wool/mohair mix.

Bottom row: fabrics include mohair/cotton/viscose mix, polyester, poly-cotton, nylon mesh, polyester.

< In fashion: Virginia James, Poetry and Wrap
Man-made fibres
Synthetic fibres >

2

2 **Liberty & Co. evening coat, c.1925**

An example of an early use of rayon in womenswear. The coat is made from silk rayon jacquard and has a gold chrysanthemum pattern. The cuffs and hems are gold rayon and the collar is made from beaver fur.

Synthetic fibres

Germany was the centre of the chemical industry until after the First World War when the USA took over their chemical patents and developed their inventions. DuPont was one of the large chemical companies developing fabrics at this time. In 1934, DuPont was able to produce long polymeric chains of molecules, the first being the polymer nylon. This marked the beginning of the development of synthetic fabrics.

Nylon is a strong, lightweight fibre, but it melts easily at high temperatures. It is also a smooth fibre, which means that dirt cannot cling easily to its surface. During the Second World War, silk supplies from Japan were cut off, so the US government redirected the use of nylon in the manufacture of hosiery and lingerie to parachutes and tents for the military.

1 **Stella McCartney for Adidas**
The shorts here are made from ClimaLite®, a fabric developed to increase comfort in exercise garments and designed to draw moisture away from the skin. The three-quarter-length tights are designed with ventilating mesh inserts and sweat-releasing fabric. Soft flat-lock seams prevent chafing when exercising.

1

< Man-made fibres
Synthetic fibres
Developments in fabric >

2

There are several other synthetic fabrics. Acrylic – developed by DuPont in the 1940s – has the look and handle of wool, is non-allergenic, but melts easily under heat. Lastex is an elastic fibre, but loses this quality after repeated washing; it is used in Spandex, which is a super-stretch fibre. Polyester is a strong, crease-resistant fibre that was developed in 1941 by ICI. It can be recycled from clear, plastic drink bottles. Acetate has the look, but not the handle, of silk. It does not absorb moisture well, but is quick to dry.

Synthetic fibres are best blended with natural fibres to improve their qualities; for example, polyester mixed with cotton will produce a fabric with a natural handle that creases less. Lycra and Spandex can be mixed with other fibres to give a stretch quality so that a fabric retains its shape with wear. It is especially suitable for performance sportswear.

2 **Second World War**
Stockings were in short supply during the Second World War as nylon was being used to produce parachutes and tents. In this photograph, women flock to get sub-standard artificial silk stockings.

Developments in fabric

Many modern developments in fabric have come from research into military use or space travel. For example, the Gore-Tex® brand was first developed as light, efficient insulation for wire on Neil Armstrong's early space mission. It was then developed and registered as a breathable, waterproof and windproof fabric in 1976, and used in the astronauts' suits in the NASA mission in 1981. It is now used widely for its properties in outerwear and sportswear.

Developments also come from looking at nature. Spider silk is naturally stronger than steel, and is stretchy and waterproof. Biochemists are currently studying its structure and developing synthesized fibres with the same properties that will then hopefully be used for fabric production.

Exciting innovations integrating technology into fabrics are being developed in the form of smart textiles, which respond to the environment through heat, wind, light and touch, for example. The basic construction of a woven or knitted fabric creates a network through which data can be transferred.

More companies are looking to produce ethical sustainable fabrics; whether that is by recycling fibres into new fabrics, recycling dyes during a dying process or by using fair trade factories in production.

1 **Apl.de.ap's graphic equalizer jacket**
Designed by Studio XO for The Black Eyed Peas' 2011 world tour, as part of a commission from Philips Lighting with their chief design officers Rogier van der Heide and Marc DeVidts, and B.Åkerlund, the band's stylist.

2 **Fergie's LED catsuit**
Designed by Studio XO with support from Philips' chief design officer Rogier van der Heide and B.Åkerlund.

3 **Taboo's full-colour LED gilet**
Designed by Studio XO with support from Rogier van der Heide, Marc DeVidts and B.Åkerlund.

1

3

2

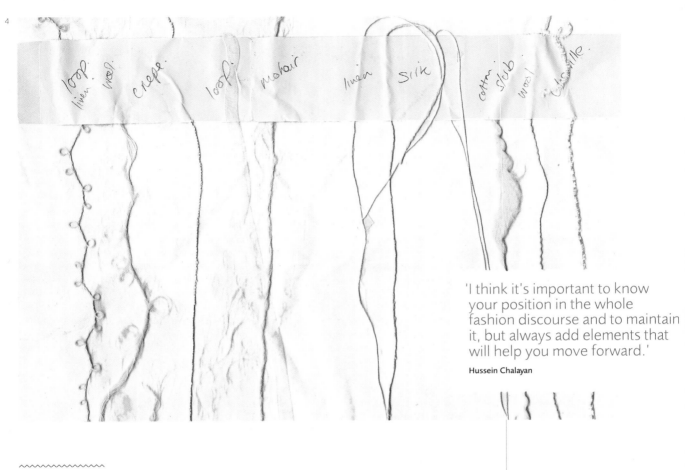

loop. linen wool. crepe. loop. mohair linen silk cotton slub wool chenille

'I think it's important to know your position in the whole fashion discourse and to maintain it, but always add elements that will help you move forward.'

Hussein Chalayan

~~~~~~~~~~~~~~~~~
Yarn production

During fibre production, man-made fibres are put through a spinning process in which they are forced through small holes in a showerhead-style structure, creating long, continuous fibres called 'filament' fibres. Unlike with natural fibres, manufacturers can control the thickness of the fibre, which is called the 'denier'.

Staple fibres are short, natural fibres; an exception to this being silk, which naturally develops in a continuous length. Filament fibres can be cut to resemble staple fibres and so mimic the properties of natural fibres. Synthetic fibres are cut down to become staple fibres when they are blended with natural fibres.

After spinning, the fibres are twisted together to form yarn. Yarn can be twisted in various ways to produce different effects in the finished fabric. Crêpe yarn is highly twisted, producing a crinkled surface in the finished fabric. A bouclé yarn has an irregular pattern of loops, or curls, along its length; fabric made from this yarn has a characteristically knobbly surface.

4 **Types of yarn**
Left to right: linen loop; wool loop; crêpe; tape; mohair; linen; raw silk; silk; cotton slub; wool slub; chenille.

Fabric construction

Woven fabrics

A woven fabric is made from a warp that runs down the length of a fabric and a weft that weaves across the breadth of the fabric. The warp and weft are also known as the 'grain'. The warp is put on the loom and is stretched taut, the weft is then woven across these warp yarns and as a result there is more 'give' or elasticity across the width of the fabric. Garments are normally cut with the major seams running parallel to the lengthwise grain or warp; this helps to control the structure of the garment. The 'bias' is at 45 degrees to the warp or weft. Garments can be cut on the bias or cross, which gives characteristic drape and elasticity to a garment.

Weave construction

The way in which the warp and weft are woven together produces a variety of fabrics. The three main types of weave construction are plain, twill and satin.

Plain weave is constructed from a warp and weft that is similar in size. During weaving, the weft passes over alternate warp threads to create the fabric and it is usually closely woven. Plain weaves include calico, flannel and chiffon, and variations to the plain weave include basket weaves, ribs and cords. Basket weave is achieved by alternately passing a weft under and over a group of warp.

With twill weave, the weft is woven over at least two warp threads before it goes under one or more warp threads; where this is staggered down the length of the fabric, it produces a diagonal weave effect. Gabardines, drills, denims, tweeds and herringbones are good examples of twill weave.

Satin weave has visible sheen and feels smooth; this is due to yarn lying across the surface of the fabric. The warp is woven to lie on top of the weft or vice versa.

Variations on the three basic weave structures include:

Pile fabrics: these are woven with yarns that are 'looped' during weaving; they can then be cut, which is characteristic of corduroy, or left as loops – for example, with towelling.

Double cloth: this is the result of weaving two interconnected cloths at the same time. Velvet is commonly woven as a double cloth – that is, cut apart after weaving to produce two fabrics that are the same. Double cloth construction can also produce a fabric made of two quite different qualities. This kind of fabric is reversible so that either side can be used as the outer layer of a garment.

Jacquard weaving: this is a complicated weave system in which warp and weft threads are lifted or left to produce patterns and textures. Jacquard weaving includes brocade and damask constructions.

1 **Warp and weft**
This diagram illustrates the warp and weft, or 'grain', in fabric.

2 **Weave**
This illustration shows the basic weave structure.

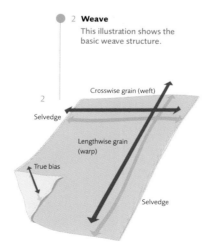

1

2

Crosswise grain (weft)

Selvedge

Lengthwise grain
(warp)

True bias

Selvedge

Wrong and right sides

Most fabrics have a front (or 'right') and a back (or 'wrong') side, the front being the side that is usually cut to be visible on the outside of the garment. The 'selvedge' is the edge of the fabric running down the length or warp so that it does not fray.

3

3 **Fabrics showing different weave construction**

From the top, left to right: wool herringbone, polyester satin, plain cotton; silk satin, jacquard, silk organza; cotton velvet, double cloth wool, denim; cotton rib, wool twill, silk chiffon. All on a corduroy background.

Knitted fabrics

Knitted fabrics are constructed from interconnecting loops of lengths of yarn, which can be knitted along the warp or weft, giving the fabric its stretchy quality. Horizontal rows of knit are known as 'courses' and vertical rows as 'wales'. Weft knitting is created from one yarn that loops and links along the course; if a stitch is dropped, the knit is likely to ladder and run down the length of the wale. Hand knitting is a prime example. Warp knitting is more like weaving; the construction is more complicated and the fabric is less easy to unravel.

Originally, knitting was produced by hand, but for many years it has been made by machines for mass production. The yarn can be knitted flat as a length of fabric or in a circular way, producing a long tube that can be fashioned to fit – knitted socks are an example of fully fashioned machine knitting. Shima Seiki and Stoll are the main producers of electronic industrial machines that can produce 2D and 3D knitting. They are highly complex models and can produce garments with few or no seams.

5

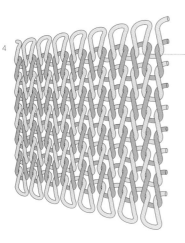

4

4 **Basic knit structure**
An illustration showing basic knit structure.

5 **Sibling**
Fair Isle twin set bearing contemporary motifs from Sibling's Collection 6.

Different thicknesses of knitting can be produced according to the size of the needles and the thickness or the count of the yarn. The number of needles per inch or centimetre of construction is known as the 'gauge'. Hand knitting can produce a variety of weights of fabric and has its own 'home-made' character; it is especially suited to very heavy knits and cables.

You can produce really creative hand knitting by increasing the scale of stitches used and even leaving stitches to deliberately ladder. To create interest within the knitted textile, texture can also be created by knitting with different needles, yarn or stitches. Changing the colour of the yarn within a textile can create pattern. Aran, jacquard, Fair Isle and intarsia are all examples of pattern within knit.

Knitwear construction

Knitwear can be constructed in three different ways. First, fabric can be knitted as a length, with the garment pieces then cut and sewn together. Second, garment pieces are knitted to shape or fully fashioned, then sewn together to produce a garment. Or thirdly, a garment can be knitted in three dimensions with few or no seams.

6 **Sibling**
George drape front hooded jacket and George Army All In One – contemporary knitwear designs from Sibling's Collection 6.

7

Jersey knitting techniques

Single jersey knit has a front 'knit' and a back 'purl' and is produced when using one bed of needles. Interlock knit or double jersey is produced with a double row of needles and the knit looks the same front and back, both showing a knit stitch.

Sweatshirting is a heavier knit, the back of which is looped. The loops can be left looped or brushed to achieve a fleece back.

Ribs and other textured knitting are produced using two beds of needles knitting alternate knit and purl stitches. Ribs can be used to finish garments on the cuffs or waistband where a garment needs to be gathered in; they have a greater stretch due to their construction. Rib can also be used to produce a whole garment.

7 **Machine-knitted fabrics**
Top to bottom: interlock (showing knit stitch front and back); loop back sweatshirting; rib (showing alternate grouped knit and purl construction); and single jersey (showing knit and purl stitches).

8 **Kaoru Oshima**
Outfit designed for FEEL THE YARN competition held at Pitti Filati, Florence in July 2012 as part of Oshima's MFA in Fashion Design & Society at Parsons The New School for Design, New York.

8

Non-woven fabrics

Non-woven fabrics are produced by compressing fibres together with the use of heat, friction or chemicals. Examples of this are felt, rubber sheeting and techno fabrics such as Tyvek®. Tyvek® is produced by matting fibres together to make a paper-like fabric. It also has a coating that makes it tear-proof, water-resistant, recyclable and machine-washable. However, non-woven fabrics needn't be man-made. Leather and fur might be considered natural non-woven fabrics, for example.

Non-woven fabrics can be used for fashion garments, but are also used for linings, padding and the interiors of shoes and bags. Due to their construction, non-woven fabrics do not fray or unravel in the same way as woven fabrics.

Other fabrics

Some fabrics cannot be classified as either woven, knitted or non-woven in construction. These include macramé, crochet and lace. Macramé is constructed through the ornamental knotting of yarn, lending the fabric a 'handcrafted' appearance. Crochet stitches are made using a single hook to pull one or more loops through previous loops of a chain; this construction is then built up to form a patterned fabric. Different from knitting, it is composed entirely of loops made secure only when the free end of the strand is pulled through the final loop. Lacemaking produces a fabric that is light and open in structure. The negative holes in lace are as important as are the positive stitches in the overall pattern of the fabric.

9

It's happened...the paper dress!

9 **Paper dress**
The 'paper caper' dress was produced by Scott Paper Company in 1966 as a promotional tool, available by mail order.

10

10 Junya Watanabe
This Spring/Summer 2012 collection featured various exquisite lace and embroidered dresses. Here, the edge of the lace is used as a natural hem to the dress.

Surface treatments

Once a fabric has been constructed, it can be enhanced or altered through a range of surface treatments. Techniques include print, embellishment, dyeing and wash finishes.

Print

Pattern, colour and texture can be applied to fabric by printing. Fabric can be printed by various methods, including screen, block, roller, mono, hand or digital printing.

Screen-printing

Screen-printing requires a design, ink, squeegee and a 'silk screen' – a piece of silk stretched evenly across a frame. A stencil of the design is applied to the screen, blocking the silk so that the ink can only pass through the 'positive' areas of the design. The screen is placed onto the fabric and the ink is pulled evenly through the screen with the squeegee, leaving a printed image on the fabric, which is fixed onto the fabric with heat so that it won't wash off. Multicoloured designs are created by using new screens for different colours. Designs are repeated by moving the screen down the length of fabric and reprinting.

Block printing

A design is applied to a hard material – such as wood, lino or rubber – by embossing or cutting into the surface to make a negative image. The block is coated with ink and applied to fabric to form an imprint.

Roller printing

This produces a continuous design on a fabric so is useful for making a repeat image over a large print area. It enables seamless printing, making joins in the design invisible, and is a faster way to produce a repeat print than is screen-printing.

Mono printing

Mono printing produces a single, unique print. Inks are applied onto a surface that is then transferred to the fabric, in reverse, to make a print. Hand painting occurs directly onto the fabric using tools such as brushes and sponges, giving a 'handmade' feel. This can be a slow process for producing a long length of fabric, however.

Digital printing

Digital printing can be applied directly to fabric from a computer via an inkjet printer. Depending on the inks used, some fabrics must first be coated with a fixative before printing. The fabric is then printed, steamed (so that the ink penetrates the fabric) and washed to remove the coating; giving the fabric a good handle, quality of colour and detail of print. Fabrics can also be digitally printed without the fixative coating, but the inks used for this stay on the surface of the fabric and the result is not such a good handle.

Heat transfer

Heat transfers use a dye sublimation process; inks are applied to paper by hand or digitally and images are heat transferred onto the fabric in reverse by a heat press. The best results are obtained using synthetic fabrics or a synthetic mix due to the inks used, which fuse with the fabric to give a good handle, and excellent colour and brightness. A different process of image transfer can be used on cotton fabrics, for example for T-shirt printing, but the image sits on the surface of the fabric.

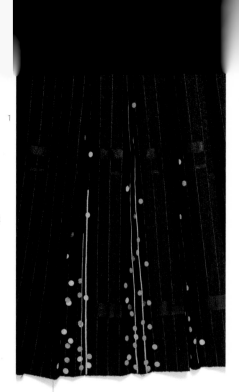

1

1 Hidden print
Screen-printed oil-based print by Jenny Udale. The print is applied within the pleats in the skirt so that the design can only be seen when the pleats are open.

2 Comme des Garçons
The Comme des Garçons Autumn/Winter 2012 collection featured felted garments with bold prints.

Printing dyes and agents

To print a colour, a dye is used with an oil- or water-based thickening agent, which stops the dye from bleeding in the design. An oil-based ink is more opaque and heavy and tends to sit on the surface of the fabric. It is available in a range of colours and finishes, including pearlescent, metallic or fluorescent. Water-based inks produce fabrics with a better handle as the thickening agent can be washed out after the fabric has been printed and fixed.

A fabric can also undergo 'discharge' printing. First, the fabric must be dyed with a dischargeable colour. The fabric is then printed with a substance that bleaches away (or 'discharges') the dye. Discharge printing is useful if a pale-coloured image is required against a dark background.

In addition to colour, texture can be achieved on fabrics via printing methods. Chemicals can be used to produce a 'relief' effect on the surface of the fabric or to 'eat away' the fabric for surface interest. Expantex is a brand of chemical that when printed and heated produces an embossed effect on fabric. Fabrics can also be printed with glue, then heat-pressed with flock paper. The flock adheres to the glue, giving a raised 'felt' effect. Glitter and foil can be similarly applied to produce special effects. Fabrics constructed with both natural and synthetic fibres within the warp and the weft can be printed with a devoré paste. When heated, the paste burns away one of the fibres, leaving behind a pattern where the other fibre remains.

Print and design

Designs can be applied in a repeat manner to a length of fabric or as a placement to a specific part of a garment. A design does not necessarily need to be just on the front or back of a garment. It makes for an interesting effect when a printed design works around the body and affects other design elements, such as the placement of seams. In this way, the print is integral to the construction of the garment.

Computer software can enable a designer to plot in a pattern piece and 'engineer' or position a print in a specific area of a garment, which can then be digitally printed in the exact position. The print can also be digitally rescaled to fit different sized garments.

Embellishment

Another way to add surface interest to fabric is to embellish rather than print, giving a more three-dimensional and decorative look than printing. Techniques for embellishment include embroidery, appliqué, cutwork, beading and fabric manipulation.

Embroidery

Embroidery can be used as an embellishment on the surface of the cloth to enhance the look of the fabric. Contemporary embroidery is based on traditional techniques. Hand stitching is the basis of these, and once you have learnt the principles, you have the foundation for a vast array of techniques. There is enormous scope for developing basic stitches. You can achieve fascinating textures and patterns by working in different threads, changing scale and spacing, working formally, working freely and combining stitches to make new ones. The key is to always be as creative and innovative as possible.

Machine embroidery can be worked on domestic or industrial machines. The machines can be used creatively and flexibly to produce a wide range of effects and techniques, from controlled to more freestyle work. As with hand embroidery, the techniques can vary in accordance with the choice of thread and fabric.

Embroidery can be applied before or after the construction of a garment, and concentrated in specific areas or as part of an overall design. Embroidery can be used in a way that makes it integral to the function of the garment, rather than simply as a decorative enhancement. For example, a buttonhole can be created with interesting stitch work and a simple garment can change shape through the application of smocking.

Devoré

Devoré is a printing technique that produces a burnt-out image on a fabric that is a mixture of man-made and natural fibres. The devoré paste burns out either the man-made or the natural fibre.

3

4

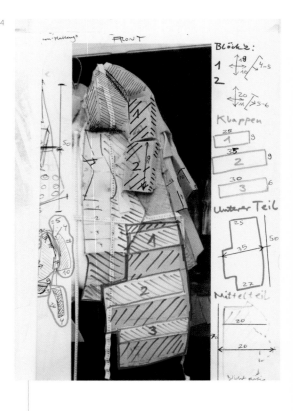

3–4 Michael Kampe
From Michael Kampe's exploded view collection. Inspiration was taken from exploded view drawings and blueprints from engineers, as well as from modern art. Image 4 shows a drawing used to work out the placement and direction of digital print on an exploded parka (image 3).

Beading

Beading is essentially embroidery with beads because each bead is attached to the fabric with a stitch. Beads can be made from glass, plastic, wood, bone and enamel, and are available in a variety of shapes and sizes. These include seed beads, bugle beads, sequins, crystals, diamanté and pearls. Beading adds texture to fabric; using glass beads on a garment lends the textile a wonderful, light-reflecting, luxurious quality. French beading is the application of beads stitched with a needle and thread on the front of a fabric. Stretching the fabric over a frame can keep the fabric taut, making beading easier and giving the work a more professional finish. Tambour beading is a technique whereby beads and sequins are applied with a hooked needle and a chain stitch from the back of the fabric. It is a more efficient way to apply beads than French beading.

Appliqué

Appliqué means to stitch one piece of fabric to another for decorative effect. Fabric motifs, such as badges, can be beaded or embroidered first and then appliquéd on to the garment with stitch.

Cutwork

Fabrics can also be enhanced through the use of hand cutwork, where areas of the fabric are cut away and stitch is applied to stop the raw edges from fraying. Cutwork can also be created by the use of a laser; more precise patterns can be achieved with laser cutting. The laser also seals, or melts, the edge of man-made fabric with heat, which stops the fabric from fraying. An 'etched' effect can be achieved by varying the depth of the laser cut into the fabric.

5

5 **The tambour hook**
This is used for applying beads and sequins with a chain stitch from the back of a fabric.

6

6 **Richard Sorger**
Details of beaded garments by Richard Sorger.

7
8

7–8 **Stefanie Nieuwenhuyse**

In this collection, the designer created a sustainable garment using natural patterns and shapes, also known as bio-mimicking. By combining modern techniques such as laser cutting with hand-sewn details, Nieuwenhuyse has created a garment with a luxurious appeal without depleting any natural resources.

1 Research
2 Design
3 Fabrics and techniques
4 Construction
5 Developing a collection

Dyeing

Most fabrics are woven or knitted before they are dyed with synthetic or natural dyes. Natural dyes are derived from plants, animals or minerals. For example, red dyes can be produced from crushed cochineal beetles or the roots of the madder plant. Most natural dyes need a fixative to stop the colour bleeding from the fabric through wear or washing.

Towards the end of the nineteenth century, fabric manufacture expanded at a rapid pace due to the Industrial Revolution in Western Europe, predominantly in the UK. Great quantities of natural resources were needed to produce the dyes for the fabric. In some cases, the natural dyes were shipped from abroad, which was expensive and time consuming. As a result, chemists started to look at ways of producing synthetic 'copies' of natural dyes. At this time, a purple dye called Tyrian purple was used to colour cloth used by royalty; it was a difficult and expensive colour to produce as it was extracted from the mucus of molluscs. A young chemist named William Perkin invented the first synthetic purple dye, which was called aniline purple, or mauveine. His discovery made him very wealthy and paved the way for the research and development of other synthetic dyes. Today, synthetic dyes are developed continuously to improve their colourfastness and performance.

Dyeing techniques can also be used to create pattern. A popular method is resist dying, which can be achieved in many ways, including batik and tie-dyeing. The latter involves tying fabric in knots before dyeing, which prevents dye from penetrating the cloth in certain areas. When the fabric is untied and dried, undyed areas form a pattern on the fabric. Tie-dyeing has an interesting history. It has been used since ancient times – the Japanese call it 'shibori' – but it was popularized in the West by the craft revival of the 1960s.

Garment dyeing

Fabric is usually dyed in lengths, but it is possible to dye garments after their construction. It is important to first test the cloth for shrinkage; dyeing often requires high temperatures to fix the colour properly, and the heat can cause the fibres to shrink. It is also important that the thread, zips and trims of the garment will react to the dye and not resist the dyeing process.

Fabric finishes

Fabric finishes can be applied to a length of fabric or to a garment that has already been constructed. Finishes can alter the look of the fabric; for example, a garment can be stonewashed to produce a pale, faded effect. Finishes can also give the fabric an added function; for example, a fabric can be waterproofed with the addition of a coating of wax.

9 **Issey Miyake**
This 100 per cent polyester garment was cut and sewn two-and-a-half to three times larger than the final article. It was then heat pressed with thousands of tiny permanent pleats.

9

Wash finishes

Stonewashing was a hugely popular finish in the 1980s and was the fashion style of choice for numerous pop bands of that era. Stonewashing uses pumice stones to fade the fabric, but it is difficult to control and can damage both the fabric and the machinery that is used to finish it. Acid dyes were later introduced to perform the same task and the effects are called snow or marble washes, but this type of process is not environmentally friendly.

Enzyme washes or bio-stoning are less harmful to the environment. Various effects can be achieved, depending on the mix and quantity of enzyme used within the wash. Enzyme washes can also be used to soften fabrics.

Garments can be sand- or glass-blasted using a gun to target specific areas where fading and distressing is required. Lasers can also be used to produce precisely faded areas on a garment.

Washing or heat can be used to give fabrics a creased or crinkled effect. Fabrics can be randomly creased by washing and leaving them unironed. Creasing and fixing the fabric before washing can form crinkles in specific areas. How long these creases remain in the fabric depends on the process used, the fabric chosen and the heat of the wash; for example, permanent creases can be made on synthetic fabrics through the application of heat, which affects the structure of the fibres.

Aromatic fabrics can be created by washing the fabric with a perfume; this process is currently being developed for lingerie. A successful way to permanently fix the smell to the cloth has not yet been developed so the perfume eventually washes out.

Coating finishes

'Coating' finishes are applied to the surface of the fabric. Fabrics can be waterproofed by applying a layer of rubber, polyvinyl chloride (PVC), polyurethane (PU) or wax over the surface. These fabrics are ideal for outdoor wear and footwear. Teflon-coated fabrics also provide an invisible protective barrier against stains and dirt – useful for practical, easy-clean garments. Breathable waterproof fabric is produced by applying a membrane containing pores big enough to enable perspiration to escape, but small enough to stop moisture droplets from penetrating.

When selecting fabric for a breathable waterproof garment, the fabric properties must be considered. Gore-Tex® is a superior example of this kind of fabric and is often used in sportswear. Cotton would allow the body to breathe, but would become damp in the rain. A PU-coated fabric would stop the rain, but retain perspiration against the body. A fabric such as Gore-Tex®, however, both allows the body to breathe and protects from the rain.

10

Denim is loaded into machines for wash finishes at 7 For All Mankind.

Fabric and yarn trade shows

Fabric trade fairs are held biannually in line with the fashion calendar (see pages 170–171). The fairs showcase new developments in fabrics and present samples from manufacturers and the mills. Designers visit these shows for inspiration and to choose fabrics for their designs. Swatch books and fabric hangers are made by the manufacturers and designers select their fabrics from these. Sample lengths of fabrics are made and sent out to the designer. The designer will then produce the garment samples for a collection and shops will place orders from these. The orders will all be collated and the fabric requirements worked out. The designer will then order the fabric lengths needed for production. If a fabric supplier does not receive enough orders on a fabric, they may not put it into production.

1 **Swatch book**
A range of fabrics from Liberty & Co. are mounted together into a swatch book.

2 **Fabric card**
Shirting fabrics of various colours, stripe widths and weights are mounted together for designers to easily access and order from.

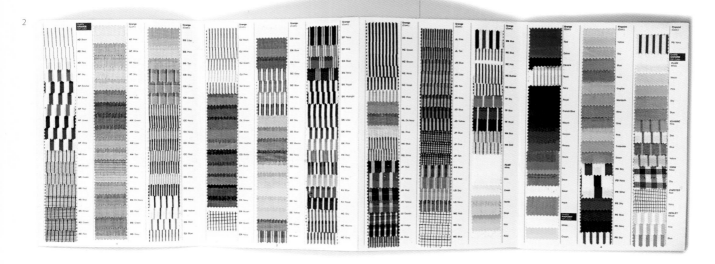

The main knitting yarn fairs are Pitti Filati in Florence and Expofil in Paris. The main fabric fairs are Moda In in Milan, Interstoff in Frankfurt, Intertextile in Shanghai, and Première Vision in Paris. Première Vision also holds fairs in New York, São Paulo, Shanghai, Beijing, Moscow and Japan. The printed textile fair, Indigo, is held at Première Vision. Fabric suppliers must sell fabrics in minimum lengths, so bear this in mind when visiting the fairs. For many students, it is simply not realistic to buy from the fairs. It is important to check the prices carefully and to find out whether there are hidden costs, such as delivery or supplement fees. Many suppliers will also require a VAT number.

3–7 Première Vision

The fashion industry visits this biannual fabric fair in Paris in order to look at new fabrics to order and to gain future trend ideas for fabric, texture, pattern and colour.

In fashion:
Michele Manz, 7 For All Mankind

What was your career path to your current job?

MA Royal College of Art; 1998–2004 – head designer at Alberta Ferretti; 2004–05 – creative director of womenswear at John Varvatos; 2005–09 – senior director of womenswear Converse by John Varvatos; 2010–present – creative director at 7 For All Mankind.

What do you do on an average day?

Depending on the day, it can include anything from calendar meetings, fittings, brainstorming, fabric appointments, sketch reviews, working on colour palettes, problem solving, styling the line, merchandising the line, presenting the line, budget reviews, meeting vendors, photo shoots, interviews and travelling for research.

How big a collection do you work on and how many collections do you design a year?

I work on twelve deliveries per year comprising men's and women's denim, sportswear and accessories. Denim usually has about six wash groups per delivery, each in a variety of styles from skinny to flare leg, as well as new fashion styles; and then about six non-denim bottoms which range from printed five-pocket styles to Tencels and various seasonal novelty fabrics. Sportswear is usually around 30 SKU's (Stock-Keeping Units) per delivery; shoes and bags about 10 per season.

How do you start to design a collection? Is research important? Where do you start?

The most important thing for 7 For All Mankind is innovation in fabric and wash, so our initial inspiration comes from the newness found at the Japanese and Italian mills that we work with as well as from experiments at our wash houses. We also take a lot of inspiration from emerging trends and interpret them into denim. Once we have a strong denim foundation, we layer on the sportswear. Research can be anything from vintage swatches and garments, street fashion, catwalk influences, exhibitions, nature and architecture.

Where do you source your fabrics from?

Première Vision and Preview NY; we also work very closely with a few select denim mills in Italy, Turkey and Japan to develop new constructions and exclusive items. We often go on fabric sourcing trips to Asia and Peru, as well as working with full package vendors domestically. The senior designers in each area are responsible for seeing many of the mills and I help to direct and edit the choices.

Is it interesting working with denim? Or do you find it restricting?

I think that denim is actually one of the most interesting fabrics to work with as it's become the foundation of most people's wardrobe. You can beat it up, bleach, tint, coat, over-dye, print, glaze, laser and stone it, and the results are always unique and interesting. Every season, I'm amazed at how much the technology within premium denim evolves and how many new techniques and washes you can execute on it. I don't believe that any other fabric has that kind of versatility.

How much of your work is travelling?

A lot! It's an important part of our business to stay on trend and be relevant. I travel to Asia two to three times per year, which includes Hong Kong, Shanghai, Beijing and Tokyo for factory, mill and store visits. I go to Prèmiere Vision in Paris twice per year for fabrics and stores. I fly to New York once or twice each month, and London and Milan (where our European head office is based) every two or three months.

Are you involved in the branding of 7 For All Mankind?

Yes, I'm heavily involved in terms of labelling and trim direction, as well as working closely with our ad agency on how our ad campaigns look and the visual team on how stores are merchandised.

What kind of team do you work with?

I have 15 designers, five pattern makers and a personal assistant report to me, and externally give direction and meet with our licensee businesses of eyewear and shoes. I work very closely with retail, merchandising, sales and marketing internally.

The best and worst parts of your job?

Worst – too many meetings, not enough time to be creative. Best – denim will never go out of fashion!

Any advice you would give someone wanting a job in your area of fashion?

Work your way up… because then you really know what you're talking about. Spend time in the wash houses. Be super-creative but relevant – keep your eye on designer trends and work on a great portfolio. Save samples of your washes or vintage pieces and take photos to create an archive. Learn as much as you can and make good working relationships… the premium denim world is very small!

Fashion file

Michele Manz is creative director of 7 For All Mankind. 7 For All Mankind launched in Los Angeles, California, during autumn 2000 and was the first company to bring premium denim to scale, marking Los Angeles as denim's centre for research and development worldwide.

The company continues to grow and evolve as a true denim lifestyle brand, expanding its product line to include women's, men's, kids', sportswear, handbag and footwear collections.

The brand's offerings also continue to expand through innovative collaborations with highly regarded designers such as The Great China Wall, Zac Posen, Azzedine Alaia, Evan Yurman and Pucci. Exciting partnerships that push the envelope of design and creativity are now a signature part of the brand's identity.

The brand is currently sold in its own retail stores, www.7forallmankind.com, luxury department stores, and high-end speciality boutiques in over 80 countries throughout the world.

1–2 **7 For All Mankind**
The 7 For All Mankind store in Santa Monica, USA.

—● 1 Research
—● 2 Design
—● **3 Fabrics and techniques**
—● 4 Construction
—● 5 Developing a collection

Fabric exercises

From reading this chapter, you should now have come to understand that fabrics come from either natural or synthetic sources, and that they are made using various processes. You will have seen that fabrics are chosen for their 'handle' (how they feel), for their performance and how they look, and whether they are used for creating silhouette or drape.

Exercise 1

Creating your own 'fabric library' is an invaluable way to begin to understand fabrics and, more importantly, how to communicate types of fabric or yarn to other designers and manufacturers. You should aim to be confident in identifying both the fabric composition and construction, for example, cotton drill or wool melton, and so on.

You will now need to conduct further research to create your own fabric reference book. Visit fabric shops, but also thrift stores to find unusual examples. By following the steps below, you should be able to create a comprehensive library of your own.

Collect together natural-based fabrics and yarn, including:

- cellulose fibres, such as cotton and linen
- protein fibres, such as wool, cashmere, angora, mohair and silk
- other fabrics, such as fur, leather and metal.

Collect fabrics and yarns that are man-made, but which use a natural source, and then fabric and yarns that have been synthesized from chemicals:

- cellulosic fibres, such as Rayon, cellulose acetate and Tencel
- non-cellulosic or synthetic fibres, such as nylon, acrylic, polyester and Spandex.

Collect yarns that have been processed to create specific effects, such as:

- crêpe
- bouclé
- slub
- chenille.

Collect together fabrics of different construction, including:

Woven

- plain weave: ribbed, basket weave, seersucker, calico, canvas, chambray, chiffon, gingham, muslin, organdie, voile
- twill weave: denim, drill, herringbone, tweed, houndstooth
- satin: crêpe-back satin, sateen, satin
- pile: corduroy, towelling, velveteen
- patterned weave: brocade, damask, jacquard, piqué
- double-faced fabrics: melton, velour, velvet

Knitted

- construction: single jersey, double jersey or rib, hand knit
- stitch interest: cable, lace stitch, tuck stitch, intarsia, jacquard

Other construction

- macramé
- lace
- crochet
- non-woven (plastic).

Cut your examples into small samples and create an organized file. Remember to only attach the fabric from the top and not to stick it completely down; this will enable you to feel the fabric and to look closely at how it is constructed at both the front and back.

1

2

1 Plain weave structures

Top row: plain weave; plain weave with chintz finish; basket-weave waffle; rib. Middle row: cotton voile; georgette; silk organza; chiffon. Bottom row: seersucker canvas; chambray; gingham.

2 An assortment of weave structures and fabric types

Top row: jumbo cord; needlecord; cotton velvet; silk velvet. Middle row: wool double cloth; cotton-spot weave with cut threads; dobby patterns; ripstop. Bottom row: crêpe; resin-coated cotton; moleskin; jacquard.

3
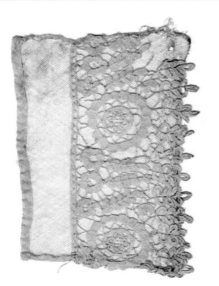

4

3 Lace

Lace sample.

4 Fabrics made from cellulose and protein fibres

Top row: Fur; leather; (woven fabrics) – wool; 50 per cent hemp/ 50 per cent cotton; raw silk; cotton. Bottom row: (knitted fabrics) – wool; cotton; silk; linen; printed silk.

5

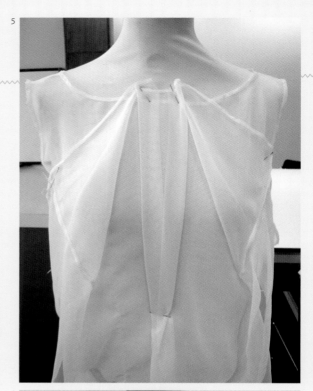

Exercise 2

Using larger lengths of fabric, start to work on the stand to create garment concepts, such as shoulder/sleeve ideas or an idea for the front of a dress. Notice how different fabrics work in different ways. You will soon be able to categorize fabrics by the way that they are constructed, the fibre used and the way they handle and also by the way that they look on the stand (for example, sheer, drapey, structured or stretchy).

- It is important that you don't try to force a fabric to do something that it doesn't want to do! Thick wool melton will be hard to drape. Chiffon will not be structured enough for a shape that stands away from the body. Experiment with what different types of fabrics naturally want to do on the stand or body (having said that, rules are sometimes made to be broken!). Photograph what you are doing on the stand for future reference too.

Exercise 3

As well as photographing this stand work, draw the fabrics that you are working with. It is important that you learn how to depict and visually communicate different types and textures of fabric. All too often the garments in a fashion illustration look like they are all made from cardboard!

- Practise drawing the following different kinds of fabric: transparent, hairy, thick, padded, leather, shiny, smooth, knit....
- Draw with a pencil, varying the pressure that you use; also vary the tone and mark making.

6

5–6 Stand work showing garment concepts being worked through.

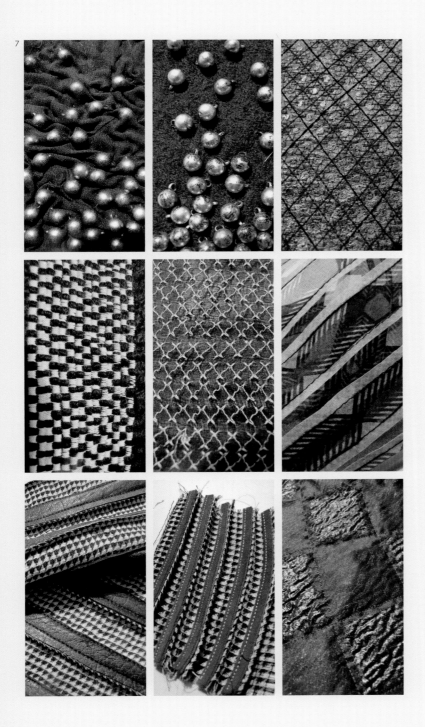

7

Exercise 4

How can you create your own fabrics from simple basic fabrics? By working into them, you will create your own interesting, original fabrics. You may also make a cheap fabric look very expensive with a bit of effort.

Try some of the following processes to create something new:

- cut
- fold
- tuck
- tuft
- stitch
- pleat
- shrink
- bleach
- stiffen.

7 **Annie Ovcharenko**
Textile experimentation including beads trapped in chiffon, machine stitching and pleating.

In context:
Marni

In this chapter, we have looked at how a designer can create their own original fabrics. For example, the fabric can be made from scratch by knitting it from a length of yarn, or an existing fabric could be personalized through the application of a print or embroidery. Using an original fabric can allow a designer to create a very specific look that is different from that of other designers. Some designers are known for their distinctive use of fabrics which help to create their own look – whether it is knit, embroidery or print, or a mixture of some of these together. Kenzo, Dries van Noten and Marni are examples of such designers.

The Marni label was created in 1994, when Consuelo Castiglioni started to make untraditional fur coats from her husband's fur business. The business grew into a fashion label as she later made garments to be worn with these coats.

Marni now has 320 points of sale around the world, with nearly 100 standalone stores in cities including Milan, London, Paris, Madrid, New York, Los Angeles, Las Vegas, Miami, Moscow, Tokyo, Seoul, Sydney, Singapore, Hong Kong, Shanghai, Beijing and Dubai.

Marni has a strong identifiable look – one that is eclectic and bohemian but at the same time thoroughly modern; silhouettes are loose and interestingly cut, and seams are often shifted forward or back so that the garment sits oddly on the body. Fabrication is key to the Marni look, especially the use of print, which often clashes with embroidery and knit, and all are seen together in one outfit. The textiles are experimental but they always remain wearable and extremely desirable. This is achieved by crafting them from the best-quality fabrics and keeping an easy silhouette, so that they are never over the top.

By creating such personal textiles, each collection is very of the moment, which makes the buyer want it for the season but also makes them desire the next clever idea in next season's collection.

The colour palette that Marni uses is very unusual, often using 'off colours' and mixing tones in unusual ways. For Spring/Summer 2012, Marni had many fabric ideas within one collection; a palette of lemon, pale blue and a bright fuchsia were used as block colours in whole outfits, or mixed together in a psychedelic floral print; nude organza underskirts peeked out under dresses and skirts; a sharply striped top was worn with an A-line leather skirt, panelled with a design of bold overlapping circles and so beautifully crafted that the patch pockets lined up identically with the pattern on the skirt beneath. In another outfit, bold African-inspired graphic crochet panels were applied on to the front of shift dresses, giving the illusion of a dress worn on top of another dress. Skirts with a wide layer of huge floral sequins at the hem were worn with a simple T-shirt-shaped geometric print top.

For Autumn/Winter 2011, the collection featured a more subdued colour palette with highlights of colour in print and beads. The look was less eclectic; 'I want to go back to the start, with simplicity and discipline,' Castiglioni said before her show (www.style.com). Small graphic prints and patterns were seen in vintage-inspired silhouettes, the patterns getting larger and bolder in looser shapes as the collection progressed on the catwalk. Marni showed fur cuffs and collars on dresses and block-coloured fur coats, some dyed a forest green and others shaved or panelled into a diamond pattern.

1

2

2 Autumn/Winter 2011
A small graphic print works on a beautifully cut dress.

3 Spring/Summer 2012
A crocheted and beaded panel appliquéd onto the front of a plain dress from Marni's Spring/Summer 2012 collection.

In fashion:
Kristin Forss, Marni

What was your career path to your current job?

I studied dressmaking and pattern cutting but it was not until I took a course in menswear tailoring that I knew I wanted to work with menswear. After college, I worked for three years for a Swedish label called Filippa-K. My job was product-based and I decided I wanted to push myself more on the creative side. I moved to London and in my second year at Middlesex University, I met the head designer at Marni and he offered me two weeks' work experience during the summer break to help him with garment patterns. I did this and was then offered a job! This was a great opportunity that I couldn't turn down even though I was about to start my final year at college, so I had to juggle working at Marni and my studies at the same time. I have now worked for Marni for nine years.

How big is your team and what are their roles?

My position is head of menswear. I work closely with a consulting stylist. We do the research together and she works with me on the big fittings and the final looks. I report directly to the head of design/owner of Marni, Consuelo Castiglioni.

How many collections do you work on in a season?

I work on two mainline menswear collections a year and four denim capsule collections for men and women.

What role does research have in your design practice? Do you enjoy doing research?

Research works as a reference point to go back to when I feel lost. I enjoy doing research, it's for myself and does not necessarily have to speak to other people. Even if I desired to stay true to the concept, it would not justify an ugly jacket.

What inspires you?

It can start with a feeling, or a picture evoking a feeling. It is an ongoing discovery during the whole process of making the collection. Along the way, the ideas get tested and sometimes it is better to admit when things are not working. I believe it is a good thing not to be too precious about your ideas.

At what point do you research fabric? And at what point in the design process do you begin to work on your fabric ideas?

We always start with fabrics, it is one of the most important parts of the collection. And of course, colour and prints. At the same time, I draw illustrations until I think I've got something that feels right. I am not naturally drawn to colours, but it is something that I have had to learn to use. Because of time pressure, I have to design during a short period of time and I usually work early in the morning and in the evening because during the day I have to do more practical work. I design by drawing technical drawings; it is not a must where I work but I have found that it is the best way for me.

1–3 **Autumn/Winter 2008**
Key looks from Men's Fashion
Week in Milan, Italy

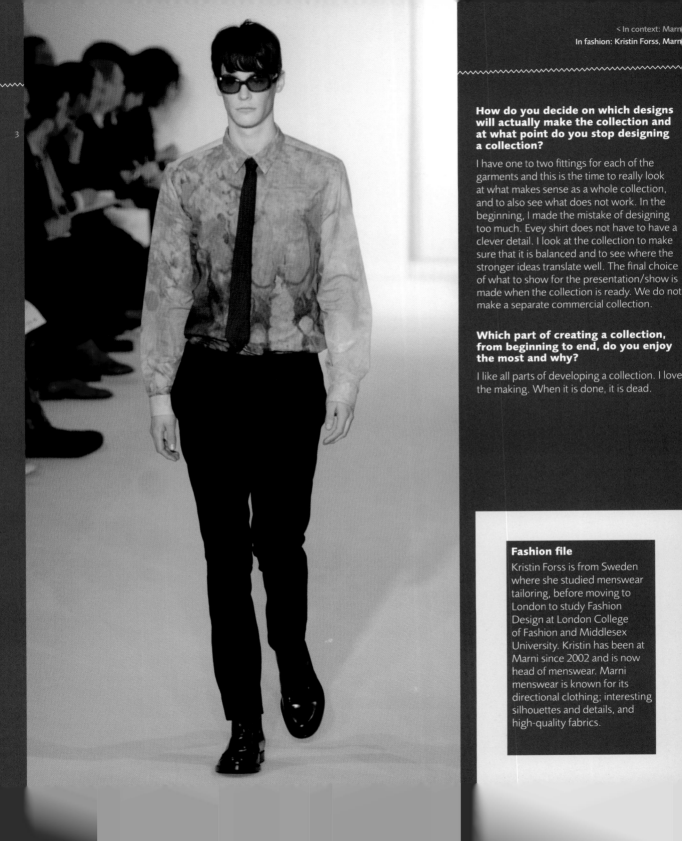

3

How do you decide on which designs will actually make the collection and at what point do you stop designing a collection?

I have one to two fittings for each of the garments and this is the time to really look at what makes sense as a whole collection, and to also see what does not work. In the beginning, I made the mistake of designing too much. Evey shirt does not have to have a clever detail. I look at the collection to make sure that it is balanced and to see where the stronger ideas translate well. The final choice of what to show for the presentation/show is made when the collection is ready. We do not make a separate commercial collection.

Which part of creating a collection, from beginning to end, do you enjoy the most and why?

I like all parts of developing a collection. I love the making. When it is done, it is dead.

Fashion file

Kristin Forss is from Sweden where she studied menswear tailoring, before moving to London to study Fashion Design at London College of Fashion and Middlesex University. Kristin has been at Marni since 2002 and is now head of menswear. Marni menswear is known for its directional clothing; interesting silhouettes and details, and high-quality fabrics.

4 Construction

Construction is the foundation of clothing and fashion design. As this chapter demonstrates, it is both a technical and a design issue; garments need seams and darts in order to render a two-dimensional fabric into a three-dimensional piece of clothing, but how and where a designer chooses to construct these lines also affects the proportion and style of a garment. The use of different types of seam is often dictated by the choice of fabric, but can also be design-led; for example, because welt seams (see page 124) are commonly used on denim clothes, they give a garment a workwear feel. A 'deconstructed' seam (a seam shown on the outside) or a raw edge, where appropriate, gives a purposefully 'unfinished' look.

It is important that every fashion designer knows and understands how garments are made. A designer must know, for example, the various possibilities of pocket or collar construction, or where a seam can go. It is only when you know the rules that the rules can be broken to innovative effect.

This chapter introduces you to the fundamentals of construction, taking you through the different types of tools and machinery required and their function in the construction process. It will also look at different sewing techniques, and techniques such as pleating and gathering that are employed to give form, volume and structure in clothing.

● 1 Research
● 2 Design
● 3 Fabrics and techniques
● 4 **Construction**
● 5 Developing a collection

Tools and machinery

Before we can talk about the methods for constructing garments, we must first look at the array of tools and heavy-duty machinery involved in the process of construction. Listed below are some of the key tools.

Tools

1 **Pattern master**

This is used for creating lines, curves and for checking angles.

2 **Tracing wheel**

This is used to trace a line from one piece of paper or pattern on to another directly underneath.

3 **Tape measure**

You can't begin working as a designer without one of these! Used for taking measurements of the body, as well as to measure around curves on a pattern if a pattern master is not available or is too short.

4 **Tailor's chalk**

Using tailor's chalk is one way of making lines or transferring a pattern onto cloth.

5 **Pins**

Pins are used to temporarily fix pieces of cloth together before they are stitched.

6 **Shears**

Large scissors for cutting cloth are referred to as shears. Never use shears to cut paper as this will blunt the blades.

7 **Rotary cutting knife**

This circular blade is used to cut fabric. Some people find it easier to cut around a pattern piece with one of these than with shears.

8 **Small pair of scissors, or snips**

A pair of these is useful for cutting threads or notches.

9 **Set square**

A right-angled triangular plate for drawing lines, particularly at 90 degrees and 45 degrees.

10 **Metre rule**

A 100cm (40-inch) ruler is very useful for drawing long, straight lines.

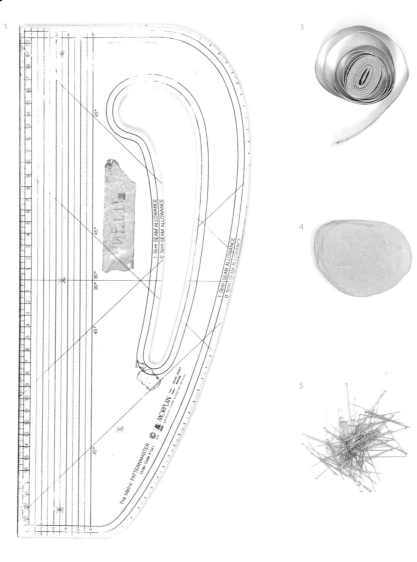

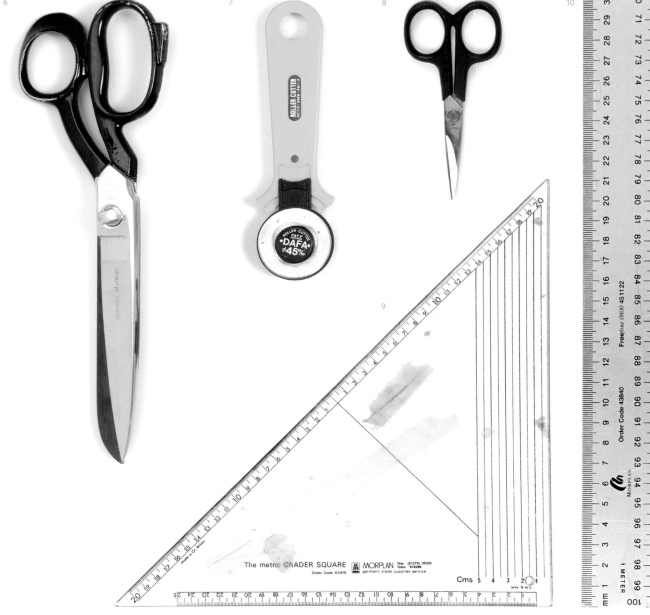

Machinery

Most designers' first experience with a sewing machine is with a 'domestic' machine. A domestic machine is useful to own as a student, but the quality of stitch will never be as good as an 'industrial' sewing machine and it is much harder (if not impossible) to sew certain fabrics, such as leather, with a domestic machine.

Industrial flat-bed machine

This machine does the basic straight stitch used to construct most types of seam. It can sew anything from chiffon to leather, but different types of fabric often require different fittings for the machine and a change in the width of the needle. For example, finer fabrics need finer needles.

Overlocker

An overlocking stitch is a series of threads that combine to create a stitch that literally 'locks' the fabric along its edge, preventing the fabric from fraying. A blade runs along the edge of the fabric, chopping off excess material and threads. Overlocking stitches can be made up of three, four or five threads and the type of fabric dictates which to use.

Overlocking stitch is used in three instances:

- On woven fabrics to prevent fraying.

- On knitted stretch fabrics as a method of creating a seam. The overlocking stretches with the fabric and therefore does not break, unlike a running stitch from a flat bed machine, which has no give.

- A superlock stitch is a dense version of an overlocking stitch and is used on fine fabrics such as chiffon.

Coverstitch machine

A coverstitch machine is used primarily in the construction and finishing of jersey fabrics and for lingerie. Twin needles create two rows of stitching on the right side of the fabric and an overlocking stitch on the wrong side of the fabric. A variation of this stitch creates an overlocking stitch on both sides of the fabric. Unlike an overlocking machine, this machine does not cut off excess fabric.

Buttonhole machine

This machine creates two kinds of buttonhole: a 'keyhole' and a 'shirt' buttonhole. Shirt buttonholes are the most common type and are used in most instances where a machine-made buttonhole is desirable. Keyhole buttonholes are mainly used on tailored garments, such as coats and suit jackets.

Industrial iron and vacuum table

An industrial iron, as opposed to a domestic iron, is heavier, more durable and the steam has a higher pressure. It can be used with a vacuum table, which is shaped like an ironing board and often has a smaller board for ironing sleeves attached. A pedal underneath the machine allows the user to create a vacuum while ironing; the air and steam are sucked through the fabric into the bed of the machine. This reduces the steam in the atmosphere and also holds the fabric to the ironing board, allowing for easier pressing.

Pressing is essential when working on a garment; fabric will crease and rumple as it is handled and manipulated under a machine. Unpressed seams do not lie flat and the garment will look unfinished if it is not ironed.

11 Industrial flat-bed machine
12 Overlocker
13 Industrial iron
14 Fusing press

11

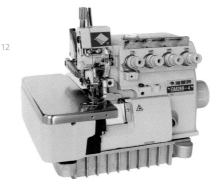

12

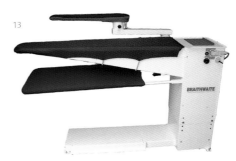

13

Fusing press

Fabrics sometimes need more substance and support; for example, cuffs and collars need more body and support than do the rest of a shirt. A fusing press is the industrial machine used to attach (that is, bond) iron-on interfacing to fabric and is more efficient and durable than using an industrial iron.

15 **Keyhole buttonholes**

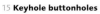

Keyhole buttonholes on an Antonio Berardi jacket.

14

Construction techniques

Seams

Making a seam is one of the most fundamental skills that you will learn as you begin to study construction. A seam is created when two or more pieces of fabric are joined together. 'Seam allowance' is the border around a piece of cloth beyond the stitch line. This extra fabric is allowed in order to create a seam. There are various types of seam and each has a specific use and purpose.

Running seam

This is the most common seam: two pieces of cloth are joined together using a flat bed machine. The seam allowance is either pressed open or to one side (seam allowance: 10mm+ (0.39 inches+)).

French seam

This is so-called because it originated in Paris, the home of haute couture ('high sewing'). This type of seam is used on fine and transparent fabrics to create a neat finish. It involves two rows of stitching; the first is completed on the right side of the fabric and the second line 'traps' the first on the wrong side (inside) of the fabric (seam allowance: 13mm+ (0.51 inches+)).

Welt seam

This is the seam commonly used on jeans, jean jackets and other types of denim garments. Two pieces of fabric interlock to form a strong and durable seam. Because of the way the seam is constructed, one side of the fabric will have two rows of stitching and the other side will have one row (seam allowance: one side 7mm+ (0.28 inches+), the other side 17mm+ (0.67 inches+)).

1 **Denim construction**
A Levi's® denim jacket constructed using welt seams and top-stitching.

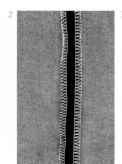
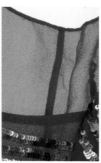

< Tools and machinery
Construction techniques
Draping on the mannequin >

Finishes

Once the seams of a garment have been constructed, the question of how to 'finish' the garment must be addressed. The finish of the garment is exactly that: the completion and tidying of raw edges, necklines, hems and cuffs, and the use of top-stitching or not. How one finishes the garment affects the overall style of it, so the choice of the finish is an important element of its design.

Top-stitching

Any stitching visible on the right side of a garment is referred to as top-stitching. It can be decorative, but its main function is to reinforce a seam.

Ordinary hem

An ordinary hem is an allowance of fabric that enables the hem to turn up either once or twice to finish a garment (for example, a hem with a finished depth of 10mm (0.39 inches) will have 20mm (0.79 inches) fabric allowance if it is turned up twice). Hems at the bottom of trousers, skirts, dresses and coats are deeper (at least 30mm (1.18 inches) finished depth).

Pin hem

A pin hem is a very short turned-up hem used to finish fine fabrics, such as chiffon or other silk. These are sewn either by machine or by hand.

Facings

A facing is used to finish edges, such as necklines or front/back openings. It looks better than turning the fabric in on itself and stitching it down and allows the finish of a garment to be completed without top-stitching. A facing is usually cut from the same cloth as the outside layer.

Hand sewing

There are various techniques and stitches used in hand sewing. Both tailoring and haute couture employ a wide range of hand stitching in the construction and completion of garments. Each type of stitch has a specific role, whether it is used for hems or for attaching canvas to a jacket front.

Binding

A binding is a bias strip of fabric or jersey which is used to neaten a raw edge. It can be used at necklines, cuffs and hems, but also as a method of neatening the raw edges of an internal seam when overlocking would be unattractive. It is considered to be a finer way of finishing a seam, but it is more time consuming and thus ultimately more expensive.

Ribbing

Ribbing is a knitted band used to finish necks, cuffs and hems of jersey garments, such as T-shirts and sweatshirts. Ribbing can also be found on garments such as bomber jackets, where it is used to insulate the wearer from the weather.

Lining

A lining is used when it is uncomfortable for exposed seams to be next to the wearer's skin. Many outerwear garments also need to be lined. This is often to 'hide' the internal construction from view: interfacings, hand stitching, canvas, and so on. A lining also adds warmth to a garment. When lining a garment, it is not necessary to overlock the inside seams.

8

2 Running seam with overlocked edges.

3 French seam and pin hem.

4 Ribbing on an Azzedine Alaïa top.

5 The inside of a Basso & Brooke jacket showing the facing and lining.

6 Ordinary hem on a pair of jeans.

7 Bias binding around the neck of a Richard Sorger dress.

8 **Tailored construction**
Section of a tailored jacket using hand stitching for construction purposes.

9

Raw edges and deconstruction

In the 1970s, Japanese designers Yohji Yamamoto and Rei Kawakubo of Comme des Garçons were the first designers to show 'deconstructed' garments on the catwalk. Their clothes revealed the seams of the garment on the outside rather than hidden on the inside. The concept was to show exactly how the garments had been put together. Raw, unfinished hems and edges can also be employed. There is no practical reason for doing so; it is purely aesthetic.

Distressing

The premature ageing of fabric is called distressing. This type of garment finish has been used in theatrical costume for a long time, but recently, so-called 'aged' garments have become fashionable. Distressing a new garment can make it look vintage or it can take away the box-fresh crispness of some clothes, such as jeans. Garments are usually distressed after they have been made. This way, the area of distress can be controlled and look more realistic – for example, on the knees or elbows. One of the techniques used to distress clothing is to machine wash it with stones.

The easiest way to distress clothing after it has been made is to wear it (and not be too careful) or to wash or boil it a few times. The fabric can also be 'aged' by applying sandpaper or a wire brush to the surface, thereby distressing it. The garment can be left outside or in a window for other 'weathered' effects. Designer Hussein Chalayan buried his graduate collection in his garden and covered it in iron filings to achieve a distressed effect.

9 **Distressed jacket**
A distressed vintage Levi's® jacket. A new collar and back yolk have been stitched in to replace the originals.

< Tools and machinery
Construction techniques
Draping on the mannequin >

Tailoring

Bespoke tailoring is the male equivalent of haute couture; clothes are made to fit the individual rather than being mass-produced to fit a standard size.

Tailoring is a term that generally refers to a method of making clothes that requires a more handcrafted approach. A good suit requires much of its work to be done by hand instead of, or in addition to, solely by machine. The fabric is manipulated and shaped through the use of hand stitching, canvas and subtle padding to create structure and form; the fabric is thereby 'moulded' to fit the form of the human figure.

Darts

One of the basic concepts of pattern cutting is rendering something essentially flat (paper, fabric) into something three-dimensional.

Darts create fit. They are triangular, tapered or diamond shapes that, once folded out of a paper pattern or fabric, convert a two-dimensional shape into a three-dimensional form. Imagine a circle; by cutting out a triangle from it and then folding it, the two-dimensional circle becomes a three-dimensional cone. By suppressing fabric, the dart helps to shape or mould fabric to the form of the body. Darts commonly point towards the bust and from the waist towards either the hips or bottom.

The placement of darts (and seams) on the body is very important; not only do they create fit, but they can also add to the style and design of the garments.

12 **Inside tailoring**
Semi-constructed tailored jacket, showing shoulder pads and the hand stitching and tacking stitches that a tailor uses to mark out important lines on the garment while it is being made. The pockets are tacked closed to prevent them from sagging.

12

10–11 **Curved darts**
Basso & Brooke jacket from the Autumn/Winter 2005 collection, with a dart that curves from the side seams towards the bust.

10

11

Creating volume

In clothing terms, volume refers to excess fabric. Creating volume in a garment means that, strictly speaking, it no longer follows the human form and alters the silhouette to some degree.

Using seams and darts to create volume

We create fit with seams and darts, but they can also be used to create volume. The easiest way to imagine how seams or darts are used to add volume is to visualize an image of the world as it appears in an old-fashioned atlas, illustrated flat like the skin of a carefully peeled orange. Where the curved lines of each section join, they form a three-dimensional globe. The triangular spaces between each section behave a little like darts. If we were to cut through the darts and separate each section, seams (rather than darts) would be required to rejoin them (this is how seams can replace darts). Employing seams or darts to create volume in this way offers endless possibilities for creating form.

13

14

15

13 **Pleats**
Black pleated dress with hood by Issey Miyake.

14 **Gathers**
The Meret Lurex shirt by Boudicca, Autumn/Winter 2005.

15 **Flare**
The 'Simulation' skirt by Boudicca uses a series of seams that flare to create a 'tail'.

< Tools and machinery
Construction techniques
Draping on the mannequin >

Pleats and gathers

16

There are various ways by which fabric can be pleated, gathered or folded. Box pleats, often found in the back of shirts, are two folds facing each other; scissor pleats all face the same way. Sunray pleats and the style of pleating exemplified by designer Issey Miyake (bamboo pleating) are more like permanent creases.

Gathering is a technique for bunching up the fabric either systematically or irregularly. While pleating is linear in nature, gathering can be more irregular.

Volume is created using these methods: when gathers or pleats go into a seam or are stitched down, the fabric is suppressed at that point and released at the point where it is no longer held down. Another technique similar to this is smocking; fabric is folded and then stitched at regular points to create a honeycomb effect.

Flare

To flare means to 'widen gradually'. The cut of a skirt can be flared to the extent that it becomes a full circle when laid flat. Flaring the panel of a garment gives it additional volume at either the top or bottom.

16 **Sculptural pleating**
This dress for Junya
Watanabe's Autumn/
Winter 2000 collection
uses intricate pleating
to dramatic effect.

17

Support and structure

When volume has been created, it can be left to drape or it may require support and structure to achieve its full shape. If, for example, a skirt has been flared into a circle, it will hang without any support, only exhibiting its fullness during movement. Supporting the skirt from underneath will force the skirt outwards and show more of its volume. Various techniques and materials can be used, generally hidden within the garment, to add body or support.

Netting

Netting is a light, stiff fabric used under a garment to bulk out or lift the outer garment. It offers the best support when gathered or 'ruffled'. Traditionally used to make ballet tutus and underskirts, netting supports the classic bell shape of a skirt. Without it, a skirt collapses and the volume deflates. It can also be used in sleeve heads to support gathering/pleating, or if the sleeve has an extremely voluminous shape, such as a 'leg of mutton' sleeve.

17 **Motorcycle jacket**
Leather motorcycle jacket
with protective quilting
on the shoulder and arm.

18

Raglan sleeve

A sleeve where the armhole seam has been replaced by seams from under the arm to the neckline is called a raglan. Raglan sleeves give the shoulder a more rounded appearance and are commonly used on sportswear.

< Tools and machinery
Construction techniques
Draping on the mannequin >

Padding

Padding can be used to emphasize different parts of the body and adds support to create volume. Dior's post-war (1947) 'New Look' collection used specially created pads for the hips to emphasize a strong feminine silhouette (see page 154). This look was scandalous to begin with – the use of excessive amounts of fabric was frowned upon in post-war Europe – but the look became hugely influential in the 1950s. More recently, Comme des Garçons challenged conventional silhouettes by padding the body asymmetrically and then stretching and draping fabric over the top (see page 48).

Shoulder pads

A shoulder pad gives more definition and form to a garment and creates a smoother appearance over the shoulder and collarbone. Shoulder pads can be bought ready-made, often from foam, but the better ones are made from layers of wadding sandwiched between felt or non-fusible interfacing. If a shoulder line differs from the norm, it is best to create a specific shoulder pad from the actual pattern of the garment so that the fit and form are perfect.

Although rarely used in tailoring, shoulder pads for raglan sleeves are also available. A shoulder pad for a set-in sleeve will not work for a raglan sleeve as they are very different in nature.

In the late 1980s and 1990s, shoulder pads became quite extreme (hence the term 'power dressing' which accompanied their return), before shrinking back to a respectable size, thereby enabling fabric to simply smooth over the shape of the shoulder and to hang well.

Quilting

Quilting refers to the technique whereby a thick, fibrous material called wadding is placed between two pieces of fabric and stitched through. Traditionally, the pattern of the stitching is diagonal, forming diamonds, but the stitching can also add a decorative effect. Fabric that is quilted is thicker and can be used to insulate a garment. This is usually added to a garment as a lining. Quilting is also used as a means of protection; for example, on a motorcycle jacket.

Another use of quilting is to create structure. A good example of this is Jean Paul Gaultier's iconic bra top, worn by Madonna on her 'Blonde Ambition' tour of 1990. The bra top references the conical bras of the 1950s, in which the bra is designed to give a totally false, idealized shape to the breasts.

19

18–19 **Atomic bomb jacket**
'Atomic Bomb' tuxedo by Viktor & Rolf from the Autumn/Winter 1998–99 collection. The outfit is constructed to fit over a 'pillow' of padding. The garments drape loosely without the padding, but still work together as an outfit.

20

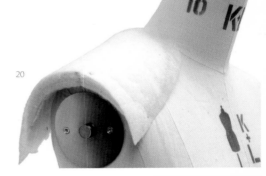

21

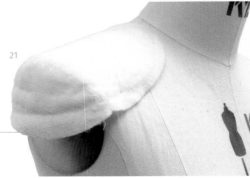

20–21 **Pads**
An example of a regular shoulder pad (top), and a raglan shoulder pad (bottom).

Boning

Boning is so-called because it was traditionally made from whale bone. It also reflects the idea of internal structure and support, like a skeleton. Today there are two types of boning: one is made of metal and the other, more common type, is made of fine polyester rods and is called Rigilene®.

Boning is used to give support to a garment, generally from the waist up to and over the bust. It can also be used to constrict the waist in the form of a corset. Strapless evening gowns, which give the wearer such great shape and – apparently miraculously – stay up, are supported internally by a corset. Vivienne Westwood's signature corset, based on a nineteenth-century style, gives the wearer instant cleavage.

As well as the corset, boning was historically used to create 'cages' suspended from the waist: a 'farthingale', worn in various incarnations between the fifteenth and sixteenth centuries, hugely exaggerated the hips; a 'crinoline', worn later in the mid-1800s, was floor-length and bell-shaped; and a 'cul de Paris' or bustle, fashionable during the late 1800s, was much smaller, but emphasized the bottom. More recently, Vivienne Westwood designed the 'Mini-Crini', which successfully married the floor-length crinolines of the mid-1800s and the risqué miniskirt of the 1960s.

Historically, boning was used to provide volume to the garment, unlike today when it is mostly used to suppress the figure; but the technique and the material used endures and is likely to continue to be used in new ways in future designs.

22

22–23 **Corset**
A Vivienne Westwood corset.

Interfacing

Interfacing is used to support and add substance to fabrics. There are two types of interfacing: fusible (iron-on) and non-fusible (sewn-on).

Interfacing is commonly used in cuffs and collars, facings and waistbands. It comes in various weights, from light to heavy, and can also be fabric-specific; there are interfacings especially for jerseys (retaining the stretch that an ordinary interfacing would prevent) and for leather (with a lower melting point).

Interfacing should be used wherever the natural tensile strength of the fabric is not sufficient to support what it is being used for.

Canvas

Like interfacing, canvas is used to give substance to fabrics. Generally heavier than interfacing and sewn in by hand, canvas is most commonly used in tailoring to give form to the front of a jacket or coat; but canvas can also be used in other types of garment where the fabric requires more body.

24

25

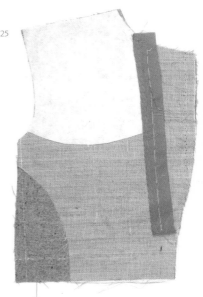

24 Interfacing
The collar on this shirt has been deconstructed to reveal the use of interfacing in the collar stand.

25 Canvas
This is the section of the canvas and interfacing that is underneath a tailored jacket.

26 Plastic boning
Fine polyester rods woven together called Rigilene® are used for boning.

23

26

Draping on the mannequin

Some clothes are too complicated or innovative to be designed in two dimensions; these ideas need to be worked out physically in three dimensions by manipulating and draping fabric on a mannequin (also called a stand). Some designers prefer to work in this manner; draping on the stand allows the designer to really experiment with forms. The possibilities of drape are arguably endless, limited only by the imagination. Understanding fabric and its properties is essential to the success of an idea worked through in this way – and vice versa. Some fabrics drape better than others and the weight of a fabric affects the way in which it will hang.

When draping on the stand, after the initial interesting voluminous forms are created, you must think about how the fabric relates to the body. Does it flatter the form? Will it move well? How do the proportions work with the body? Working in this manner can be rewarding, but also requires discipline. It's easy to create forms on the stand – but can they be converted into interesting and contemporary garments?

1

1 **Draping**
Existing garments can be experimented with on a mannequin to create new garment shapes, much in the same way as using a length of cloth.

Pattern block

All garment patterns start life as pattern blocks. A pattern block is a basic form – for instance, a bodice shape or a fitted skirt that can be modified into a more elaborate design. A designer/pattern cutter will develop their own blocks that they know and trust. Books on pattern cutting supply instructions on how to 'draft' certain pattern blocks from scratch using a list of measurements that relate to measurements of a standard (human) size. Patterns can also be taken from fabric that has been draped on a stand in order to develop a design.

Pattern cutting

Before the garment is made out of fabric, a pattern for the garment is cut out of paper. This paper pattern is then used to cut the cloth for the garment. 'Pattern cutting' is the term used to refer to this process of making the paper garment pattern.

The basic premise of pattern cutting addresses the question of how to render something essentially flat (paper, fabric) into something three-dimensional.

Good pattern cutting must be precise so that the pieces fit together accurately, otherwise the garment will look poorly made and will fit badly. An inaccurate pattern will also create problems for the person sewing the garment together.

Each pattern contains 'notches' or points that correspond to a point on the adjoining pattern piece. These are cut into the seam allowance of a piece of fabric and help whoever is making the garment to join the seam together accurately.

There are basic rules of pattern cutting that need to be learnt before the designer or pattern cutter can become more adventurous and experimental. Changing one element of a pattern can have a knock-on effect on another piece of the pattern and a pattern cutter must be aware of this. For example, changing the armhole of a garment means that the sleeve must also change accordingly.

2 **Paper patterns**
Sample pattern pieces.

1 Research
2 Design
3 Fabrics and techniques
4 **Construction**
5 Developing a collection

Dart manipulation

The dart can be moved around the body to create different lines (but a bust dart must always point towards the 'bust point' as this is where the fit and form is required). Darts can also be incorporated into seams; the seam will become shaped and curved to create fit. The placement of darts (and seams) on the body is very important; they not only create fit, but also add to the style and design of a garment.

Resolve all potential construction issues on the toile and you'll make fewer mistakes making the garment with the real fabric. Producing good toiles saves time later but you don't need to make real pockets or put a lining into a toile. A good toile should help a sample machinist to create your garment exactly as you want it.

Sample sizes

The first version of a garment made in real fabrics is called the 'sample'. It is this garment that goes on the catwalk or is shown to the press. Samples are generally made to a standard US size 4–8 (UK 6–10) to fit the models.

'Slash and spread'

This term refers to cutting a pattern at a strategic point or along a line, opening it up and adding in extra volume. Flare is often created using this method. The technique of 'slash and spread' can be used to convert a straight skirt pattern into a flared skirt (see the patterns running on this and the facing page).

Toiles

A design can look very different when converted from a two-dimensional drawing into a three-dimensional garment; proportions, details and fit may need to change so this is an opportunity to make modifications before the final garment or outfit is made.

'Toile' is French for 'cloth'. The term has been appropriated to mean a mock-up of an actual garment. It is made in a cheaper fabric – often calico (an unbleached cotton fabric, in French known as 'toile de coton') – to check fit and make. The purpose of making a toile, or 'toile-ing', is to simulate the final garment, so it is necessary to toile in a similar fabric; for instance, if the garment being 'toiled' will ultimately be made in a stretch fabric, it must first be toiled in jersey. It is essential to use a similar weight fabric for the toile, as a design cannot always be realized with certain weights of fabric; this can be resolved when toile-ing.

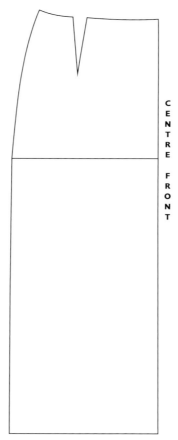

1 A basic pattern block for a straight skirt.

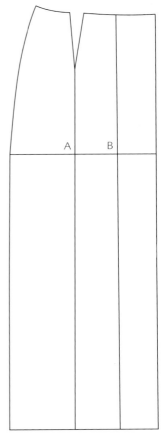

2 The pattern is divided into three sections.

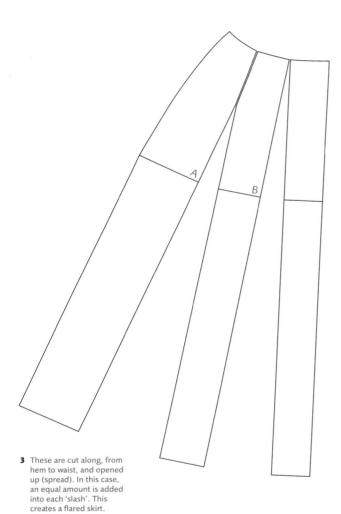

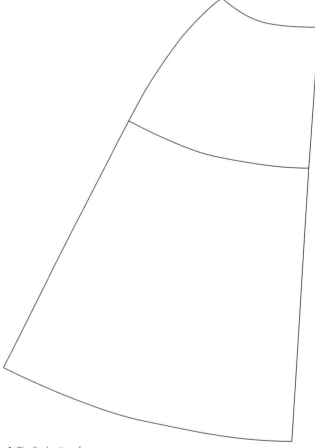

3 These are cut along, from hem to waist, and opened up (spread). In this case, an equal amount is added into each 'slash'. This creates a flared skirt.

4 The final pattern for the new flared skirt.

In fashion:
Boudicca

What was your career path to your current job?

Our path started on a windswept winter beach in Rimini (Italy). We had both been asked to work on a project together out there and had only met briefly before the trip. After many conversations in deserted bars, we both realized that we had a great deal in common; as for the subjects we didn't agree on, we both fought their causes with a similar passion and determination for the point at hand.

It was from these conversations, this initial path, that Boudicca was born – from a need to examine and investigate clothing and image. We both realized the importance of self image and both had a history of experimentation with our outward image... we then took the path less travelled.

Please describe your brand

Boudicca is a set of tensions that climb in and out of masculine and feminine, history and future, tailoring all thoughts and referenced on multiple levels, that when brought together form a new language that defines itself in the moment.

Boudicca is a combined force of strong tailored silhouettes alongside softer shirts and dresses, but it always continues to find places where the work is challenging all of this and almost surprising the initial thought... . To repeat forever can become less challenging and boring, not only to your own head in design but for the clients who support us in what we do.

Boudicca is further an exploration of both design and an expressive biography of the times we live in. Its outcome is a direct response to our ever-evolving constant questioning of our method of expression.

One of our joys and rewards from Boudicca is the very nature of the label, the constant state of flux – so even when we re-read these questions, we are constructing another answer... and the creative pendulum swings.

The idea of a clear definition fills us with the fear of categorized acceptance whilst the duality of both male and female designers contributes to what we see as the future of womenswear – an equality that is represented in dress.

Boudicca has no wish to be a clothing factory making hundreds or thousands of the same garment sold in the same store all over the world. We want to remain niche and exclusive, where a sense of discovery is part of the Boudicca experience. Wearing Boudicca should become an addiction, as you feel powerful and safe in your own personal armour, yet romantic and attached to the emotion within the garment itself. Boudicca is anti-mass.

How big is your team and what are their roles?

Boudicca is so many people. The immediate team is small but a brand is a tribe and that tribe, that team, that system, requires everyone to participate – designers, studio, consumers and clients alike.

How many collections or projects do you work on in a season?

We have shown in three capitals now; London in our early days, New York towards the end of the Ready-To-Wear shows and then on to Paris where we began the dream of further understanding the 'art of dress' during the Boudicca Couture show in Paris, where we were invited by the Chambre Syndicale.

1

1 **Lace dress**
'Nicole in dark lace',
Autumn/ Winter 2002.

2 **Boudicca Couture 2002**
Backstage photo from the
Boudicca Couture show,
Paris 2002.

3 **Tornado**
Still from the film
'Tornado. A dress' (2009),
directed by Ben Bannister.

Since then we have worked more with film, digital technologies, sculpture and three-dimensional sketches, creating montage-edited compositions that present ideas in clothing and also more abstract works built around the ideas of a collection – some more evident and some more research-based. This seems to have now become a reality for the industry and so the need to show or even produce collections in the formal way is changing and may even be eliminated as we all begin a new conversation, a new language of fashion.

Projects happen really quite erratically. This year we have been asked to be part of an exhibition in Chicago, 'Fashioning the object', curated by Zoë Ryan; we have also been invited by Mike Figgis (the film director) to participate in his creative weekend 'Deloitte Ignite' at the Royal Opera House in London.

Ongoing, we will be displaying a piece of sculpture in Ed Vaizey's office (the UK's Minister for Culture), and we still have four metal sculptures in Kensington Palace – which are still spinning after one year – in the Cupola Room. Within the last week, we have had requests to make three more films, interviews and other collaborations too.

Of course, you cannot do everything and so it is about positioning and balancing your choices. Collaborations are crucial to instigating the new. Conversation occurs and challenges present themselves when two mediums mix. It is again very true of the beginning of a century to want to break up what you know by introducing another.

What is your approach to research?

Our world is surrounded and pasted with imagery like daily wallpaper to most of our lives. And yet as people we choose to find our own landscape by researching constantly and learning, gaining knowledge about the culture all around, as well as studying the lectures of our past. That means inviting your dreams to interact with your memory of past art, philosophy, writing and poetry to find a world that you feel generally expresses the dream you have developing in your mind; and to secure your visual understanding of the world that defines all us of today.

What is your design process?

Discussion – words – thoughts – research – images – sounds – fabrics – drawings (scanned in and grouped together and cleaned-up) – patterns (the line on the pattern paper is as important as the line in any of the drawings) – paper mock-ups – toiles – digital images – drawing in three dimensions – digital images printed out and any changes drawn on top – cut up digital images and collage of different ideas and propositions – fittings – photographs – propositional changes – pattern changes – final toile in similar or same fabric in some cases – live with final toile (for a week or so) – make final garment – maybe it becomes part of the collection, maybe it waits for the next one. The whole process is an ongoing creative evolution right through to the final garment. There is no greater reward than seeing an actual rendering of an imagined idea. But please note that this order can change and will.

Boudicca is far more than just designing clothes. Please explain.

Form follows emotion: it's the unspoken language that garments have, the intimate relationship formed between wearer and garment that Boudicca examine. The design reflects that demand, is the documentation of that examination. Not clothes as escapism, but of expression within their escape. 'Clothes are not just a product, they are our armour, our silent opinion.'

What advice would you offer someone who wants to become a fashion designer?

Times are changing and the future is never something we can know or dictate... and that is the key feeling... not to know.... In fact, we need new designers to offer us all up something that breaks down what we have and take us down the path less travelled for themselves.

4

4 **Digitally printed dress**
This striking dress features a monochrome digital print and sculptured silhouette.

5

Fashion file

Boudicca is the London-based design duo of Zowie Broach and Brian Kirkby. Started in 1997, Boudicca was a purely artistic expression showing in art galleries and other exhibition spaces until 2001, when Boudicca were invited by the British Fashion Council to present officially during London Fashion Week.

Boudicca is a design house respected for its integrity, depth of design and attention to detail. It offers collections that are deeply researched and designed while beautifully executed in the finest European fabrics, all with serious attention to the fit and finish of each garment.

5 **Tuxedo**
The classic tuxedo boldly reconfigured by Boudicca.

Construction exercises

In this chapter, you have been introduced to the fundamentals of constructing garments; from the practical tools and machinery used, through to construction techniques. We have additionally looked at various methods of realizing garments, such as draping fabric on the stand to develop ideas and the use of pattern cutting to create paper patterns from which to cut cloth.

Exercise 1

As a designer, it is important that you begin to recognize the various techniques that are used to construct garments. This is so that you can make informed decisions when making your own garments or when instructing a third party as to how you would like a garment to be made.

- Go and look at clothes: in stores, your own, or from other sources. Find and photograph two examples of as many of the following as possible: running seam; French seam; welt seam; top-stitching; ordinary hem; pin hem; facing; hand sewing; binding; ribbing; lining; raw edges/distressing/deconstruction; tailoring; darts; pleats; flare; netting; padding; shoulder pads; quilting; boning.

- Now design a range of garments, five in total, each garment clearly using a combination of at least two of the above techniques or finishes. Your range should demonstrate the use of at least ten different techniques or finishes.

Exercise 2

Pattern cutting is a complicated subject that can take years to learn to a high standard. As discussed in this chapter, two of the basic principles of pattern cutting are dart manipulation and 'slash and spread'. Read the following steps about how to create a miniature front bodice in conjunction with the patterns on the facing page.

Step 1

- The dart can be moved around the body to create different lines, but in the example of a bust dart, it must always point towards the 'bust point' as this is where the fit and form is required.

- Trace out the miniature front bodice pattern onto paper. This basic pattern block for a bodice has two darts, one from the waist (dart A) and one from the shoulder/neckline (dart B).

- Cut along line D, stopping 1mm (0.039 inches) before you reach bust point (X). Do the same with line G. The pattern has not been cut into two, but is holding together by 2mm (0.078 inches) at point X.

Step 2

- 'Fold out' dart B by rotating line D to meet line E. This action causes dart A to become larger. You have now manipulated an existing dart to another place on the bodice (dart B is now incorporated into dart A), but the fit remains the same.

Step 3

- Trace and cut out the bodice that you have just created with the larger dart A. Draw a new line (C) on the bodice pattern from anywhere on the edge of the pattern to the bust point (X). (In this example, the line has been drawn from the side seam, pointing up towards the bust point X.)

Step 4

- Now, using the same process as in Step 1, cut along line C to the bust point X, stopping 1mm (0.039 inches) before you reach it. Repeat with line G, stopping 1mm before bust point X. Rotate line G to meet line F, closing dart A. As you close dart A, the dart opens out in line C thereby creating a new dart (C).

Exercise 2

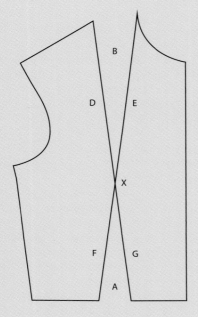

Step 1

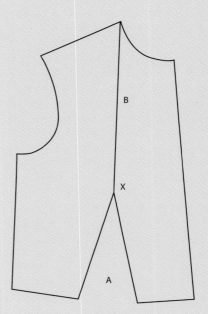

Step 2

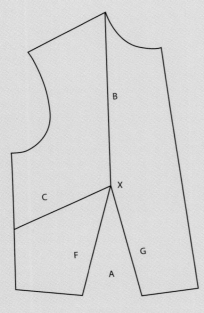

Step 3

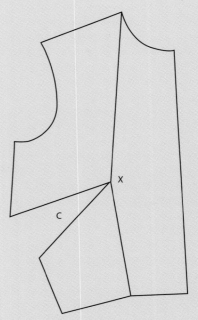

Step 4

—● 1 Research
—● 2 Design
—● 3 Fabrics and techniques
● 4 **Construction**
● 5 Developing a collection

Exercise 3

Step 1

- The technique of 'slash and spread' can be used to create volume. For example, it can be used to convert a straight skirt pattern into a flared skirt.

- Trace out the miniature front skirt block onto paper and cut out. From the bottom of dart C, draw a straight line down to the bottom of the pattern (line 1). Now draw a line halfway between line 1 and the centre front. This is now line 2. Label the three sections X, Y and Z.

Step 2

- Cut up line 1, stopping 1mm (0.039 inches) before point A. Now cut down line 3 towards point A, again stopping 1mm before point A. Next, cut up line 2 towards point B, stopping 1mm before you reach it.

- Now 'close' dart C by rotating line 3 to meet line 4. This opens out line 1. Stick down section X and Y to a sheet of paper. Measure the distance that has been opened at the bottom of line 1 (the distance between new points D and E). Move point G away the same distance as points D and E, and then stick section Z down.

Step 3

- Take a new piece of paper and trace the outline of the skirt from step 3, joining up the line to create a new flared skirt pattern. You now have a paper pattern from which you can cut cloth for a flared skirt!

Step 1

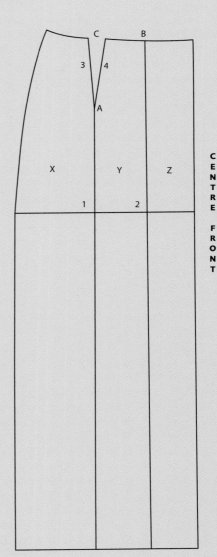

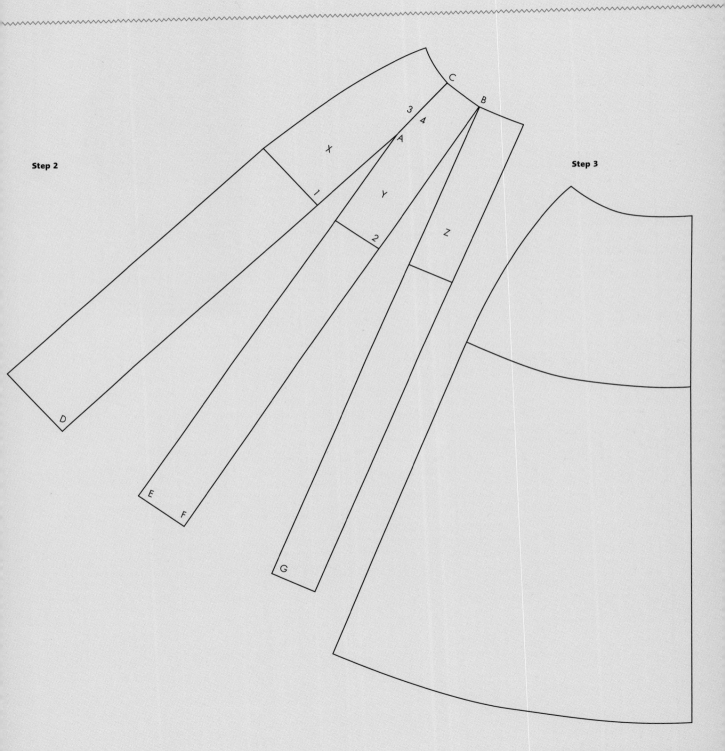

Step 2

Step 3

▶ **In context:**
Alber Elbaz, Lanvin

In this chapter, we have looked at the fundamental construction techniques used to make clothes, from creating basic seams to different techniques employed to create shape and volume.

How clothes are constructed is not only a technical issue but also a design issue; the type of seams and finishes used in the clothes affects the overall appearance of the garment and therefore the design.

One designer who excels and innovates in his use of construction is the Moroccan-born designer, Alber Elbaz, who was appointed Creative Director to the Paris fashion house Lanvin in 2001. Previously, he had worked for Geoffrey Beene, Guy Laroche, Yves Saint Laurent and Krizia.

Since then, Elbaz has expertly combined Lanvin's heritage with his own unique style to critical and commercial success, by seemingly breaking the rules of garment construction. Alber Elbaz believes that fabric should skim the body rather than cling: skimming is not only sensual but further allows his designs to appeal to all ages whilst flattering all body shapes.

His draping and the construction of his garments can sometimes be subtle and difficult to detect in photographs, and the clothes need to be seen up-close in actuality to really appreciate them. Then, they show unexpected finishes, often appearing to be partially constructed, with raw edges or exposed seams that accentuate their fragility and show a lightness of touch.

Elbaz explains his approach to design by saying that 'after perfection, there is nothing'. He understands the rules of garment construction and it is this understanding that allows him to innovate and also to 'break the rules'. In a sense, he steps back from the perfection of a garment in favour of exploring imperfection.

To create a garment 'imperfectly', Elbaz uses the technique of deconstruction, which is the tension between how a garment is finished and how it is left unfinished, partially revealing the secrets of how it is put together.

To achieve this, Elbaz will often cut dresses on the bias-grain (diagonally) – meaning that the edge of the fabric does not necessarily need to be hemmed, as a bias-cut edge will not fray.

Many designers have incorporated raw edges and deconstruction techniques, but rather than the clothes merely looking unfinished, Elbaz's subtle garments manage to achieve the effect of 'haute couture hand-me-downs'.

Through many seasons, Elbaz has popularized another deconstructed detail, the exposed zip on the back of a garment. Rather than simply concealing it in a seam, he chooses instead to let this component show.

Similarly, in Spring/Summer 2011, pleated garments revealed their darts and had seams on the outside; in the following season, the tops of the pleats on the skirt of a dress were exposed instead of being integrated into a seam.

1

● 1 **Spring/Summer 2011**
The silk chiffon fabric of
this dress skims the body
and drapes through a
collar before transforming
into the sleeve.

Jeanne Lanvin
The Lanvin label was founded in Paris in the early twentieth century by Jeanne Lanvin, who made such beautiful clothes for her daughter that she received many requests for her to duplicate her designs for other children. Lanvin's expert use of intricate trimmings, embroideries and beaded decorations in light, floral colours became her trademark. The Lanvin empire grew to include home decoration, menswear, fur, lingerie and perfume, and the designer became one of the most influential designers of the 1920s and 1930s.

2 **Spring/Summer 2009**
The draping on the shoulder of this dress looks deceptively simple, as though it has been done quickly and casually – which, of course, it hasn't!

In context:
Alber Elbaz, Lanvin

When Elbaz designs with draping, there is a lightness of touch to the way that the fabric hangs, is pleated or is gathered. Often, the fabric will look as though it has been 'tucked' in an informal manner rather than intentionally constructed in this way.

For Spring/Summer 2012, he introduced subtly padded shoulders with the fabric lightly 'tucked' around them. Discreet pleats were caught into the side seams of the skirts to create the effect of permanent folds in the fabric.

In an earlier collection (Spring/Summer 2009), the fabric was twisted and folded back on itself on the front of tops, and on some garments it was bunched at the shoulders or neckline. These details looked as if the models themselves had casually arranged them moments before walking on to the catwalk.

This 'casual' draping also appeared in the Spring/Summer 2011 collection, where draped dresses appeared to twist through a neckpiece and continued to drape around the body.

This simplicity is, in fact, very difficult to achieve; to drape something in a way that appears so simple and effortless takes talent along with a complete understanding of the fabric to be used.

3

4

3 Spring/Summer 2012
This side view shows the tucks around the shoulder pad and the exposed zip of the skirt. The skirt itself has been pleated into the zip to create drape.

4 Spring/Summer 2012
This Grecian-style dress is draped to one side and held by pins.

5 **Autumn/Winter 2011**
The sleeves of this top
appear to have been
tucked casually into
the neckline.

5 Developing a collection

Before you even start thinking about putting a collection together, you must first identify early on what kind of clothes you want to design and sell, and at what level – are you designing for men, women or children, for example? Do you want to design for the high street or for haute couture? What do you want to include in your collection? You must also understand the different types of garment and whether they can form a collection on their own or in combination. You must consider the fashion calendar and how collections fit into this timetable. Finally, you must think strategically about the different ways that you can promote and sell the collection.

Who are you designing for?

As a fashion designer, you can work at various 'levels' within the fashion industry. The choice of direction you make will depend on your training, ability and interests – as well as, of course, how much you would like to be paid for your work. Finding your niche in fashion design may be something that you've been working towards from the beginning – or it may evolve more organically. But when you do start a collection, you should have a very clear understanding of who you are designing for.

1 **Dior**
Menswear from Dior's Autumn/Winter 2012 collection.

Haute couture

The couture fashion shows are held twice a year in January and July. The shows present womenswear to potential buyers and function as advertising for the fashion houses. The instantly recognizable names of the top haute couturiers include Chanel, Christian Dior, Givenchy, Jean Paul Gaultier and Valentino.

Haute couture garments are made to fit individual customers and are very expensive, as a couturier uses the most exclusive fabrics and highly skilled artisans. Without couture, these amazing making and embellishment skills would be lost. To learn the specific rigorous skills of haute couture, you would be best advised to complete a degree in fashion design and then find a placement working in-house with a couturier. The skills required at this level are impossible to cover sufficiently during a three or four-year degree course and can take years to perfect.

Today, there are very few clients who can afford couture, but it is still an essential part of the fashion industry as the collections are innovative and original, and are less restricted by commercial restraints than are ready to wear (or prêt-à-porter) collections. Haute couture clothes push at the boundaries of fashion.

2

2 **Dior's 'New Look'**
Christian Dior's iconic 'New Look' dress from 1947.

3 **Christian Dior**
Christian Dior haute couture from the Spring/ Summer 2012 collection.

Luxury super brands

Fashion super brands are global companies. They have immense advertising budgets, their own stores and produce their own perfume and accessories. Super brands also design and sell diffusion lines under their name. They design and produce luxury designer goods and promote their collections on the catwalk during the designer prêt-à-porter shows.

The LVMH (Louis Vuitton, Moët Hennessy) group and the Gucci group are the two main fashion luxury goods conglomerates that own many fashion brands and super brands. Bernard Arnault is the president of the LVMH group, which owns Louis Vuitton, Céline, Kenzo, Thomas Pink, Emilio Pucci, Givenchy, Loewe, Fendi, Marc Jacobs and Donna Karan. François Pinault owns the Gucci group, which includes Gucci, Yves Saint Laurent, Boucheron, Bottega Veneta, Balenciaga, Alexander McQueen and Stella McCartney.

Ready to wear (prêt-à-porter)

As haute couture collections are far too expensive for much of the fashion-buying public, some designers create collections that are high quality, but which are produced in larger numbers to fit many customers within the range of standard sizes – these collections are called 'ready to wear'. Given this, they still retain an air of exclusivity. As the new ready-to-wear collections are not designed for individual customers, they can afford to reflect the designer's concepts. Ready-to-wear styles are at the top end of the fashion industry. Ready-to-wear fashion is designed by a diverse range of designers, from independent designers through to the luxury super brands.

Mid-level brands and designers

Mid-level brands or designers are not as powerful as a super brand, but they are nevertheless established companies that have been trading for a few years with a good turnover and profile. They will sell wholesale or may have concessions or franchises, and they may have their own stores. A mid-level brand or designer is usually well known within a specific area of design or within a particular country. A mid-level designer may show on the catwalk and work with a high-street store – for example, British designer Matthew Williamson, who has successfully collaborated with the UK department chain store Debenhams with his 'Butterfly' range.

Independent designer labels

An independent designer works with a small team to produce a collection. They have complete control over their business, so they are able to design very personal collections. Depending on the size of the team, they also need to be in control of all the other areas of the business including finance, sampling, manufacturing, press and sales. This can take up a great deal of time, leaving little time to design fashion, so it is crucial for the independent designer to find the right balance.

The independent designer may show his or her collection on the catwalk at fashion fairs like Prêt-à-Porter. Typically, the collections are sold wholesale to boutiques or department stores, and the designer either sells directly to them or via a sales agent. For example, designer Christopher Kane currently sells his collection to fashion store buyers at London Fashion Week and is stocked in Selfridges, London, and Barneys, New York.

Casualwear, sports and denim brands

The areas of casualwear, sportswear and denim also have super brands, mid-level and new independent labels. Brands working in these areas do not show on the prêt-à-porter catwalk but instead may promote through advertising. Nike is an example of a super brand that produces large commercial collections with a variety of sub-categories. They produce Nike 6.0 for surf; have also their tennis and NIKE RUNNING lines; and additionally own the brands Converse, Hurley and Cole Haan. They run expensive marketing campaigns and sponsor many of the top sporting celebrities and events in the world, but also do grass roots campaigning.

High street

High-street fashion companies design collections that go straight to retail. They have chains of stores or franchises across the country or even the globe, and online stores. The high-street stores look at the catwalk collections and pick up on trends, and because of their manufacturing set-up, are able to react quickly to them. They design and make garments quicker than ready-to-wear designers are able to – partly because the quality of the development, fabrics and production is less intensive. The production process from initial sketch to final garment can take weeks as opposed to months. High-street stores are not part of the biannual fashion weeks and they do not usually show their collections on the catwalk. One recent exception to this rule is Topshop, which enjoys some crossover appeal.

Supermarkets

Many supermarkets now sell ranges of clothing alongside groceries and other products. Garments are produced quickly and in bulk to satisfy the demands of the consumer, so clothes cost less to manufacture and can be sold at a very reasonable price.

4–9 **Emma Cook's Spring/Summer 2012 collection**
These patched denim pieces and *trompe l'oeil* digital denim prints are by independent designer Emma Cook.

Genre

1

Womenswear

The womenswear market is saturated with designers and is therefore highly competitive. This is probably because womenswear is considered to be not only more creative, but also crucially more glamorous than other areas of fashion.

Menswear

Menswear is more conservative than womenswear and is therefore subject to fewer and more subtle changes from season to season – for example, trouser width may alter or a collar may simply change shape. Menswear sales are also less significant. Men tend not to buy as many clothes and when they do, they are more expensive and longer-lasting. In terms of what men and women wear on a day-to-day basis, men normally wear a less diverse range of garments than do women.

Childrenswear

Childrenswear design can be just as sophisticated as womenswear and menswear but, in addition, designers must consider health and safety restrictions and the appropriateness of the garments. Childrenswear includes clothes for newborns, toddlers, kids, and teenage boys and girls.

1   **Thom Browne menswear**
From Thom Browne's
Autumn/Winter 2011–12
menswear collection.

2

2 **Chloé womenswear**
Womenswear from Chloé's
Spring/Summer 2012
collection.

'It's great to tell a story in a collection, but you must never forget that, despite all the fantasy, the thing is about clothes. And, while you are editing to make the impact stronger, you have to remember that there has to be a collection and it has to be sold. We have to seduce women into buying it. That's our role. What you see on the runway isn't all you get: That represents less than a quarter of what we produce. Merchandising is vital. We have to keep the shops stocked, looking fresh and seductive.'

John Galliano

In fashion:
Colin McNair, John Varvatos

What is your job title?

I am Design Director at John Varvatos.

What was your career path to your current job?

I previously worked at MaxMara, Pringle of Scotland, Whistles and Nicole Farhi.

What do you do on an average day?

Mostly sit in meetings! I am responsible for the younger casual line here at John Varvatos which includes leathers/outerwear/tailoring/pants/denim/knits and sweaters, so I have to coordinate my design team, the production team and overseas agents/suppliers, as well as secure licences to make sure that the collection gets done each season.

How big a collection do you work on and how many collections do you create a year?

On average, I create a 140 SKU collection across all categories per season and there are four seasons in a year.

How do you start to design a collection? Is research important? Where do you start?

I start with colour palette and imagery. It is important to be as visual as possible, as so many people have to understand and rely on what you are envisioning. Research is everything from who the customer is, colour, vintage garments, construction details, books, magazines, Internet, blogs, visiting stores and travelling to other cities/climates. There is no start... it's a constant thing that you can't turn off. There truly is inspiration in everything... even a blank piece of paper!

Research also involves past sales information and bestsellers from the past, which we either repeat in new fabrics/colours or perhaps create adaptations of. I am given this information from other departments in the company.

Where do you source your fabrics from?

Trade shows, visits to mills in various countries when travelling overseas, as well as agents visiting us in our office. We have a person who is in charge of fabric but it is part of my job to select the fabrics.

How much of your work is travelling for research or for factory visits?

A lot! I travel nearly every month.

What kind of team do you work with?

I have a team of three designers as well as a graphic designer. But design essentially oversees all parts, from the development all the way through to production, so the team that I work with always extends beyond my immediate team.

Best and worst parts of your job?

The best parts are the people and the creativity.

The worst parts are the people! And that fashion has become more about the money than the art!

1–6 **Spring/Summer 2012**
Pieces from the John Varvatos Digital Star collection.

Fashion file

Colin McNair graduated in June 2000 from Kingston University, London with a degree in fashion. He then worked for Pringle as a womenswear designer for three years, before moving to Whistles briefly as a senior womenswear designer. McNair then switched to working as a menswear designer at Nicole Farhi where he stayed for three years. Next, he moved to New York to work for John Varvatos where he has been ever since. McNair has also freelanced for both Italian and British brands at various points in his career as well as having his own hand-knitted accessory line.

4

5

6

Types of garment

Whether you design for menswear, womenswear or childrenswear, there are different ranges within each genre; for example, casualwear, jeanswear, evening wear, tailoring, swimwear, underwear, lingerie, knitwear, sportswear, showpieces and accessories. If you have your own fashion company, you will probably design all of the areas within your collection. But if you go to work for a large company, such as Hugo Boss or Gap, you will specialize in a certain area – for example, outerwear (coats and jackets) or dresses.

Casualwear

Casualwear is defined as everyday clothes that are not typically worn in a formal situation. Casualwear gained momentum in the 1950s with the evolution of youth culture. Teenagers didn't want to look like their parents and so started to dress in their own way. Designers and manufacturers responded and a more relaxed form of dress developed, which has since grown exponentially and become a global phenomenon. The two most common fabrics associated with casualwear are jersey and denim. Sportswear and underground urban style are the main influences on this area of fashion. Gap, J. Crew and Abercrombie & Fitch are examples of casualwear brands.

Denim wear

Jeans are trousers made of denim. Originally worn as clothes for manual work, they became popular among teenagers in the 1950s. Today, jeans are a truly international item of casualwear, worn by young and old alike. They are designed in numerous styles and colours. With developments in fabrics and washes every season, designers are constantly reinventing the product by producing new twists on the classic jeans. Many denim brands have evolved from simply designing jeans to designing other garments in order to give a broader product offer.

Levi's®, Lee, Diesel and Wrangler are well-known denim brands. Levi's® is a brand based on authentic American workwear. Interestingly, Levi's® has a very different status around the world; in the USA, the brand represents more of an entry price point denim, while Levi's® Asia and Levi's® Europe jeans are seen as a cool heritage denim fashion statement.

7 For All Mankind is an example of a premium denim brand (see pages 108–109). Using the best denim from fabric mills in Italy and Japan, combined with perfection in fit and wash, the jeans were the first 'dressed-up' jeans to be worn with designer clothes and were deemed chic enough to wear in the workplace. Other premium denim brands are J Brand, Citizens of Humanity, Paige and Current/Elliott, with jeans retailing at around $200 (approximately £125) in high-end department stores, such as Selfridges, Liberty & Co., Barneys and Saks.

1 **The Jean**
Top left to bottom right:
Levi's® 501XXX; Evisu
cinch-back; Levi Strauss;
high street; Rogan; Nudie;
BleuLab; Y–3.

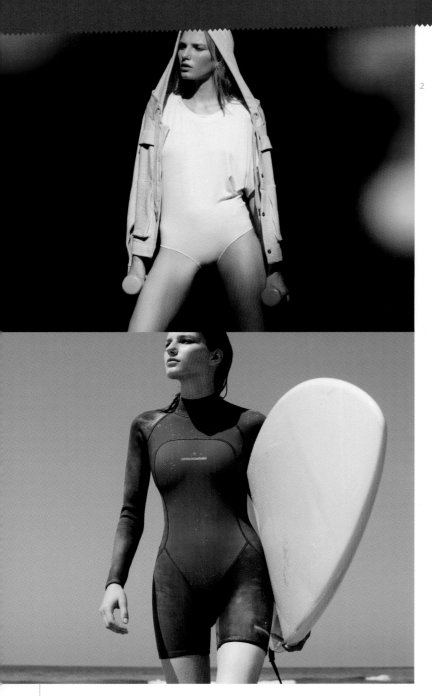

2 **Stella McCartney for Adidas**
From McCartney's Spring/
Summer 2012 collection of
'sport performance' wear.

2

Sportswear

Sportswear design is almost entirely led by function; garments must perform in relation to a specific sport or activity. Yet as fabric technology constantly evolves, sportswear has become fashionable for everyone to wear, not simply sports enthusiasts. Sportswear has its own trends, which can affect main fashion trends. This is especially apparent in trainers, where a functional trainer is adopted as a street trend, which in turn is picked up by fashionistas. Converse (owned by Nike) produces trainers initially designed for basketball players; these have since become iconic and are now also worn off the court as fashion footwear. Converse is currently working on a footwear range with the designer John Varvatos (see pages 160–161).

There are many crossovers between sportswear and fashion. Manufacturers now commission fashion designers to make functional sportswear more fashionable. Stella McCartney has collaborated with Adidas to produce 'sport performance' design collections, including garments for running, the gym, swimming and tennis. Paul Smith has worked with cycle brand Rapha and undercover with Nike on a running range called 'Gyakusou', and Cynthia Rowley with Roxy. Sportswear also influences fashion design – for example, Yohji Yamamoto teamed up with Adidas on its Y-3 collection, which includes technical sports fabrics and construction techniques, as well as the Adidas triple-stripe logo.

Swimwear

Nowadays, many people are able to holiday in hot countries at all times of the year, thus increasing the demand for swimwear. In sports, fabrication and designs for swimwear have advanced technologically, allowing for greater variety within the basic garments.

Underwear

3

Underwear design has predominantly been about technology and function, but in recent years it has become more self-consciously design-led. Agent Provocateur and Victoria's Secret are examples of companies that design functional, luxurious, stylish underwear and lingerie. Unusually for underwear companies, they show their collections on the catwalk, underscoring the importance of underwear as an area of design. Agent Provocateur has its own store and concessions, and also previously collaborated with the British retailer Marks & Spencer on a range of lingerie.

Evening wear

Perhaps obviously, evening wear is more formal than daywear. Even today, men's evening wear remains quite traditional, but women's evening wear is limited only by the imagination. One only has to consider the global media attention on the night that the Oscars are held, when the actresses and models make their way down the red carpet, to know how important evening wear is for fashion and to see how diverse the styles, colours and fabrics are.

Evening wear garments tend to be made from finer, more expensive fabrics, such as taffeta and silk. Evening wear tends to transcend seasons, and it is less easy to identify an evening gown from one year to the next.

3 **Alexander McQueen**
Evening wear from the Alexander McQueen Autumn/Winter 2011 collection.

4

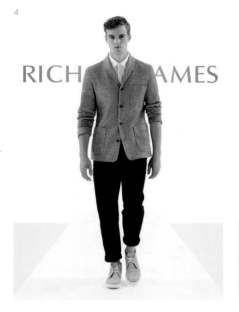

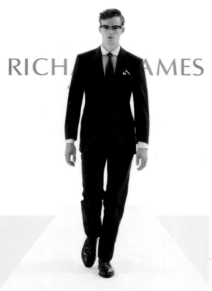

Tailoring

As one might imagine, tailored clothes have more structure and fit than do casual garments, and specific skills are required in order to understand their construction. Tailored garments are perceived as being formal and are considered to be the appropriate dress code in many places of work.

Bespoke tailoring is the menswear equivalent of haute couture. Each suit is made to fit a specific customer. Many men are still willing to pay top dollar for a well-cut suit that will last them for many years.

4 **Richard James**
Key looks from the Spring/ Summer 2012 collection by Richard James.

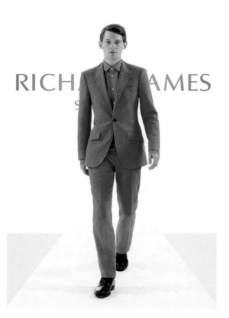

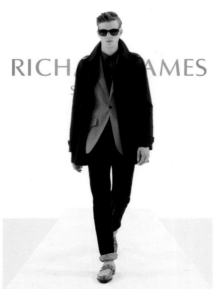

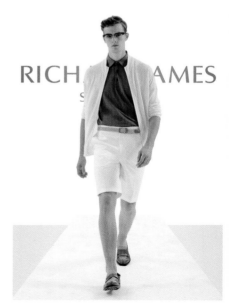

Showpieces

Within many catwalk collections, some clothes are considered to be more wearable than others, but you can always guarantee that some clothes will elicit cries from the public of 'Who would wear that?' However, what many people don't know is that these outrageous creations are called 'showpieces'. These pieces never make it onto the rails of shops or boutiques, but are conceived to attract the design press, either as part of the coverage of the show in which they appeared or when worn by a celebrity promoting the designer to a wider audience. Showpieces are intended to grab attention. They are often time consuming and expensive to make and ultimately represent the designer's undiluted vision.

Knitwear

Knitwear designers are really the only fashion designers who develop the construction of the fabric of a garment as well as its design, as they are responsible for making key decisions about the yarn, stitch and silhouette. Some fashion brands have developed from knitwear companies that have their own identifiable style. For instance, Missoni is famous for its multicoloured striped knitwear and Pringle for its diamond argyle patterns.

5

5 **Thierry Mugler**
The pop star Lady Gaga wearing a showpiece from Thierry Mugler's Autumn/Winter 2011 collection.

6 Sibling
All-in-one (grey) and fox pompom hat (red) from Sibling's Collection 6.

7 House of Flora
These hats were part of the Fashion in Motion show at the V&A Museum in London (2009). The Hat Anthology with Stephen Jones featured an acrylic flower hat, an orange pipe cleaner hat and a PVC beret.

Accessories

Accessories finish the look of an outfit. They include bags, belts, hats, shoes, scarves, jewellery and eyewear. Many brands produce accessories along with their clothing collections to offer a complete look. The customer can style themselves from head to toe in one brand if they so choose.

Accessories are generally cheaper than garments and enable consumers to buy into a brand via the purchase of a pair of sunglasses, a belt or a signature bag when they may not be able to afford the clothes. Accessories can also change the look of an outfit – they can dress it up or down. A pair of trainers with a women's outfit will look more casual than a pair of high heels, for instance.

They can also work as fashion status symbols, made desirable through media endorsement. This is especially true of bags, and each season there is a new coveted bag with its own identifiable name and look from the major fashion houses – for example, the Birkin at Hermès, named after style icon Jane Birkin, the Novak at Alexander McQueen and Alexa at Mulberry.

Footwear, hat and bag design are specific areas of design which require a great deal of skill in terms of construction, as well as design and function.

With the evolution of the celebrity hairstylist in the 1960s and 1970s, wearing hats fell somewhat out of favour. These days, there are fewer occasions for which wearing a hat might be appropriate. However, there are a few successful established milliners; in the UK, for instance, Philip Treacy and Stephen Jones produce a range of ready-to-wear hats, but also design elaborate pieces for the catwalk shows of Dior and Alexander McQueen.

In fashion:
Alan Humphrey Bennett, Bally

What is your job title?

Accessories designer for Bally.

What was your career path to your current job?

I did a BA in fashion and then decided to focus on accessories. I spent two years getting work experience in London and then started an MA in accessories; I was interviewed whilst still in college and started at a large leather goods company straight afterwards.

What do you do in an average day?

Sketching, also altering sketches as the collection is constantly changing from day to day. Materials and finishings are also always changing, so data always needs to be updated too. There is lots of work using Photoshop as well.

How big a collection do you work on and how many collections do you create a year?

I work mostly on the men's collection. We have about 10 lines and each season we may have about 100 new bags. I also work on belts, small leather goods and key chains.

Where is the collection shown?

In Milan, during Men's Week. The women's collection is also shown in Milan.

How do you start to design a collection?

The company tries to be very commercial. The merchandisers present to us the skeleton of how they see the new collection, describing new needs and functions for the market, that is, new pockets for electronic devices and required materials. This then forms the basis for the commercial collection. We receive more creative research (vintage pieces/images) from the creative directors, which we then design with for the press show pieces. We also do our own research at leather and vintage fairs across Europe. We finally pull together all this different research to create the collections.

Where do you source your fabrics from?

We have someone to do our materials research. However, the design team will still go to trade shows for interesting materials. We will later work directly with the researcher to find the right materials at the right price.

What are the essential qualities needed for your job?

Patience to deal with the demands of designing a quality product and the different people involved with this process. You need to be organized and have everything on hand at a moment's notice. There is never enough time to take long periods for research or design, so you need to keep constantly informed of both the market and also what really inspires you.

1

Fashion file

Whilst in London studying for a degree in fashion design, I worked for Meadham Kirchhoff, Roksanda Ilincic, Siv Støldal and Vivienne Westwood. I became interested in the notion of bags being objects as well as something you carry around; so I studied for an MA at the Royal College of Art, London and learnt how to make bags by hand. I then started working for Bally one week after finishing my MA. Now I live in Florence.

How creative a job do you have?

Half of the time it is very creative; the other half is basic office work.

What kind of team do you work with?

There are two of us working on men's accessories, my boss and I, which is a very small team.

What are the best and worst parts of your job?

The worst part is not always having the freedom to design what I want. The best part is seeing myself develop over a very short space of time, living in another country, learning the language and eating lots of Italian ice cream.

What advice would you give someone wanting a job in your area of fashion?

In any area of fashion these days there are so many people. I believe that tactical decisions are very worthwhile. Be honest with yourself about what you are truly really good at and what comes naturally. Focus on those skills and be the best at them. The hard thing is getting into the industry; once you are in, you meet enough people to keep you there. Most importantly though – stay excited about life!

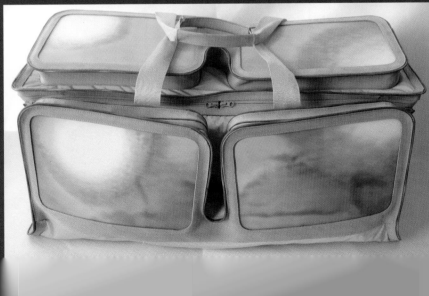

1 Research
2 Design
3 Fabrics and techniques
4 Construction
5 Developing a collection

Putting together a collection

Fashion design is a fast-moving industry. In order to succeed, you must be well-organized and prepared for a lot of hard work.

Collections and ranges

The fashion year has two seasons, six months apart. The industry works on a cycle, with one collection for the Spring/Summer and another for the Autumn/Winter seasons. Small fashion companies produce just these two collections a year, but larger companies produce more. Often, they sell two smaller collections that go in-store for the Christmas period and high summer. The Christmas collection or 'cruise' collection can include partywear or clothes for winter holidays.

The high-summer collection focuses on swimwear and summer holiday clothes.

Smaller pre-collections are produced as tasters of what is to come, and are shown to buyers just before the main collections. Designers may also produce a commercial selling collection, from which buyers primarily place their orders. This allows the main collection catwalk shows to be more experimental and so catch the eye of the press.

High-street fashion retailers introduce ranges of clothes more frequently into their stores to keep customers constantly interested. This is done by subdividing the main collection into smaller collections or 'stories' and staggering their release to the stores across the selling period.

These are easier to market and merchandise than a single, very large collection. Stories are usually given names – normally a word that sums up the theme of that story, for example: Contour, Zanzibar or Marianne.

A designer may be working on many collections at one time. For example, in January a designer may be showing a pre-collection, finishing the look of the Autumn/Winter main line collection for selling, finishing the cruise collection and starting to design the main Spring/Summer collection all at the same time. For a large ready-to-wear company, the Autumn/Winter collection may have around 200 pieces, the cruise collection 100 pieces and the Spring/Summer collection 160 pieces.

1

	Jan	Feb	Mar	April	May	June	July	Aug	Sept	Oct	Nov	Dec	Jan	Feb
Womenswear Prêt-à-Porter Fashion Year														
Spring/Summer 1	Yarn + Fabric Fairs. Première Vision. Showing Spring/Summer ideas. Start designing Spring/Summer.					Sampling Spring/Summer collection.		Samples back + finished.	Spring/Summer Fashion Weeks. London/NY/Paris/Milan.		Orders collated + order fabric + trims. Start production.		Deliver Spring/Summer collection to store.	
Autumn/Winter 2								Yarn + Fabric Fairs. Première Vision + Pitti Filati. Start Autumn/Winter designing.			Sampling Autumn/Winter collection.		Samples finished.	Autumn/Winter Fashion Weeks. London/NY/Paris/Milan.
Spring/Summer 3													Yarn + Fabric Fairs. Showing Spring/Summer ideas. Start designing Spring/Summer.	

Menswear shows are earlier, but delivery times are the same

< In fashion: Alan Humphrey Bennett, Bally
Putting together a collection
Showing a collection >

For a new independent designer, a collection might be more in the region of 20–100 pieces (15–50 outfits) in different colourways. A shirt designer for Topman, for instance, would be expected to design around 50–60 different styles of shirt a season over six stories.

1–2 **Womenswear schedule**
Calendar showing the basic prêt-à-porter fashion year. In addition to working on this, designers are likely to also be working on other collections, including pre-collections and cruise collections.

3 **The runway**
A press shot from a Peter Jensen catwalk show showing buyers reviewing a new collection.

2

Womenswear Prêt-à-Porter Fashion Year															
Mar	April	May	June	July	Aug	Sept	Oct	Nov	Dec	Jan	Feb	Mar	April
	Selling finishes. Books close.	Collate orders + order fabrics + trims. Start production.		Deliver Autumn/ Winter collection to store.									
			Sampling Spring/Summer collection.		Samples finished.	Spring/Summer Fashion Weeks.	Selling finishes.	Orders collated. Production starts.		Deliver Spring/Summer collection to store.			

Menswear shows are earlier, but delivery times are the same

1 Research
2 Design
3 Fabrics and techniques
4 Construction
5 Developing a collection

Garments designed for a season

Garments are applicable to different seasons. For example, coats are obviously more important than swimwear in the Autumn/ Winter season. Fabrics also differ; heavier, warmer fabrics are used more in Autumn/ Winter and cooler, lighter fabrics in Spring/ Summer. However, as many of us work in air-conditioned buildings and live in heated houses, the differences between seasons are becoming less apparent, and clothes are becoming less significantly seasonal. We also tend to layer clothes up so that we can wear summer pieces with sweaters in winter.

The design process in industry

As a designer working for a company, the first task in designing a collection is research. You may be involved with forms of research other than those discussed in Chapter 1. Going on shopping trips in your local environment and around the world keeps you informed of fashion and other cultural trends. Fabric and fibre fairs are important for finding out about the latest developments in fabrication. Depending on the size of the company you work for, you may have to talk with merchandisers and buyers to discuss the shopping habits of your target customer, as well as which garments have sold well and which have not from previous and current collections.

Having digested the research, the collection is designed and a range is drawn up. A specification drawing is made for each garment, and fabric samples and trims are selected. From this, a pattern is cut and sampled. The samples are assessed on their individual merits and in terms of how they work in the collection as a whole. The sample may be altered in terms of fit, fabrication and detail, and then re-sampled. The entire sampling process may take place in-house or it may be sent out to the factory that manufactures sampled clothes. The designer or other members of the team will be in charge of this process.

4
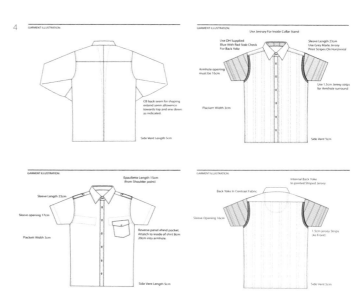

5

● **4–5 Spec drawings**

Spec drawings are working drawings that are used to communicate details of garments to manufacturers, along with shots of the finished items (images shown by Grainger).

Light Wool

Knitted Rib

Lycra

Cotton Jersey

Chunky Knit

Leather

Transparent plastic

3D tube around the head. High waisted bikini pants, mixed with a business shirt and tie.

Sophisticated Knee length pencil skirt in a light wool.With 3d tube looking tucked inside skirt.

3D tubes made as a statement of a cropped jacket. Ribbed waistband. Cotton, tailored trousers.

Detachable 3D collar around the head, in a transparent pvc fabric, showing clothes on the inside. Off the shoulder top in a light summer fabric.

Chunky knit, winter cardigan. 3D tube framing the face.

High waisted, lycra leggings. Oversized 3d shapes framing face.

Light fabric, pencil skirt. Chunky knit cardigan.

Padded jacket either grey leather or clear pvc. Lycra swimming costume underneath.

Pencil skirt in a light fabric. Chunky knitted scarf. Padded jacket.

Padded bomber warmer stuffed with clothes. Either leather or clear plastic. Classic cotton suit trousers.

Oversized 3D ring around the shoulders. Tailored trousers.

Clear ring around the shoulders showing the clothes. Slim fit trousers, with elastic around the foot

Light woollen, pencil skirt. Wider gusset on the ring, behind the back of head

Lycra swimming costume. Chunky knit scarf going around the body. 3d ring around the shoulder; stuffed with clothes.

Knee length coat. Padded shoulders. Shoulders clear plastic, jacket in leather or vice versa.

Knee length coat. Chunky knit jumper wrapped around the body.

Short sleeved, padded jacket. Top panel in leather, bottom panel in clear plastic. Cotton leotard.

6 Range plan

Range plan for signature collection by Jamie Russon.

'The constant hunger for renewal in fashion is driven not only by a commercial imperative and the consumer's delight in "newness" but also by a fascination with image and narrative.'

Claire Wilcox, curator

Showing a collection

Once a collection is designed and made, your priority is to show it to the press and buyers. It is important to thoroughly research different fashion events to find the one best suited to your product. Try and show at the same place for a few seasons as this encourages the press and buyers to get to know you and to see that you are a company that is continuing to trade season on season.

Designers generally show in the country in which they work and live – at least initially. This is because they understand their home market and because it is usually less expensive than showing abroad. As the business grows, they may start showing internationally and the cities in which they choose to do this will depend on the kind of product that they are showing and the stores that they wish to target.

There are many fashion events around the world. The main womenswear ready-to-wear shows are held during Fashion Weeks in Paris, Milan, London and New York, and the haute couture shows are in Paris. The menswear ready-to-wear fashion shows are during the mens' Fashion Weeks in Milan, Paris and New York (which are usually ahead of the womenswear shows). There are also shows that cover all the other areas of fashion, including casualwear, denim wear, underwear, accessories and childrenswear.

1

1 Preparing for the runway
Last-minute preparations are made backstage at Justin Smith Esquire.

'It's more like engineering than anything else. It's finding the limits of what you can do when wrapping the body in fabric. Everything evolves. Nothing is strictly defined.'

John Galliano

< Putting together a collection
Showing a collection
Branding >

2

2 **Hussein Chalayan**
For Hussein Chalayan's
Autumn/Winter 2000
collection, staged at Sadler's
Wells in London, models
deconstructed a stage set of
furniture and then wore the
table and chair covers.

The catwalk show

The catwalk show, or runway, is a great way
of showcasing a collection as clothes are best
seen on the body whilst in motion, thereby
displaying their fit and drape. The designer
can create a complete concept for the
collection through the styling of models and
the setting of the show itself. Press, buyers,
stylists, possible investors, sponsors and peers
are invited to the show. Buyers will make notes
on what they might like to buy for their stores.
Press will be commenting on the collection for
newspapers and magazines, as well as looking
at which pieces to use for future photo shoots.

Catwalk shows are very expensive events with
no direct financial return. The return will only
come if the collection receives good press and
if orders are taken at the showroom afterwards.
A catwalk show can cost upwards of £20,000
(approximately $32,000) so new designers
often try to secure some form of sponsorship
for their show. Some high-street retailers offer
sponsorship in return for a collection to go
in-store. It is important not to show on the
catwalk too early. If the collection is poor and
the show unprofessional it may do more harm
to a designer's credibility and bank balance
than good.

Timing and venues

Organizers of the Fashion Week shows vet designers and decide who will show on the official schedule. It is usual for new designers who are not on the official list to show 'off schedule', which means that they can show their collections, but perhaps in smaller, less high-profile venues. They may attract press and buyers hoping to discover an exciting new underground talent. Press will support a new underground designer for a while, but may lose interest if the momentum does not seem to build around the designer and his or her business. Buyers tend to wait a few seasons before buying a new designer's collection. They want to make sure that the business is established enough to manufacture and deliver a good-quality collection on time to their stores.

A catwalk show can take many different formats and there is no single rule or approach. The catwalk or runway typically runs down the centre of a large auditorium or room, with seating areas at either side with an area for the bank of photographers at the end of the catwalk. Models walk one by one up the catwalk, pose and turn to walk back. However, some designers choose to show their clothes in a more personal or conceptual way – the show being a very important part of the collection's ethos.

Designers try to find unusual venues, such as car parks, football stadiums, warehouses and subways. The designer must think about what lighting and music best suits the collection in order to create an ambience for the show. The guests' invitations and the 'goody bag' that they receive when they arrive also help to set the scene and attract the right people.

Alexander McQueen was known for his dramatic fashion shows. For Autumn/Winter 1999–2000, he staged his show (called 'The Overlook') in a huge cube containing a snow-covered landscape, with his models skating on ice. The show was inspired by Stanley Kubrick's horror film 'The Shining' (1980). He also presented a show where the catwalk was on fire, and another where he manufactured rain falling on the models.

Hussein Chalayan's Autumn/Winter 2000 show was held at Sadler's Wells Theatre in London, UK. He set the stage like the interior of a house, and the models deconstructed the furniture to create garments; tables turned into skirts, and seat covers became dresses (see page 175). Designers have also experimented with taking their collections off the catwalk altogether to show them as a film or on the Internet instead.

4

5

3–7 Boudicca show invites
Boudicca are very experimental with the invites to their fashion shows; creating everything from talking invites to an engraved false nail.

3

6

7

8

8 **Trade show**
Views of the crowded
floors at Magic in Las
Vegas, USA.

Trade shows and showrooms

Whether they have a catwalk show or not, all designers have a static display of their collection. This presentation may be at a stand, an exhibition or in a private showroom. Here the clothes can be viewed in detail by the press and by buyers who will hopefully then write orders. To attend a trade show, you must normally make an application to display your collection and hiring space can be expensive. It is possible to get government funding to show at some of the international trade shows. The ready-to-wear trade shows are part of the Paris, Milan, London and New York Fashion Weeks.

Casualwear and denim wear designers and companies usually show at the big trade shows, including Magic in Las Vegas, Pitti Uomo in Milan or Bread and Butter, which has shown in Berlin, Tokyo, New York and Sydney.

Showing your collection in a showroom can be more intimate than showing at a trade fair. The showroom can be in your own premises, in a hotel room or at your selling agent's premises. You may show alone or as part of a group. It is important that your showroom is easy to get to as the buyers and press will have many showrooms and catwalk presentations to visit in any one Fashion Week.

Selling agents

Some designers sell their collections through a selling agent. An agent can be useful as they have contacts with buyers and can arrange appointments for you. The agent charges a commission on orders placed in the showroom. If you use an agent, make sure that you ask for feedback about how the collection is selling. This advice is invaluable and can impact on your next collection.

1 Research
2 Design
3 Fabrics and techniques
4 Construction
5 Developing a collection

Look books and line sheets

A 'look book' documents the collection and is a valuable selling and promotional tool. It enables press and buyers to leave the showroom or trade fair with a detailed record of the collection that they have just viewed, which they can use for reference later.

The look book can take various forms – it may simply comprise photographs from the runway or may be something more creative.

A line sheet is a more detailed document showing all the designs as spec drawings or photographs with fabric, colour options and prices, which is very useful for buyers.

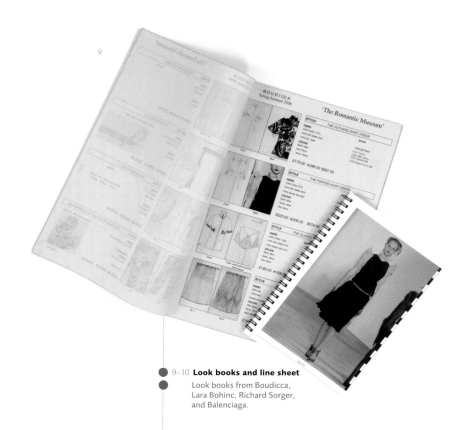

9–10 **Look books and line sheet**

Look books from Boudicca, Lara Bohinc, Richard Sorger, and Balenciaga.

< Putting together a collection
Showing a collection
Branding >

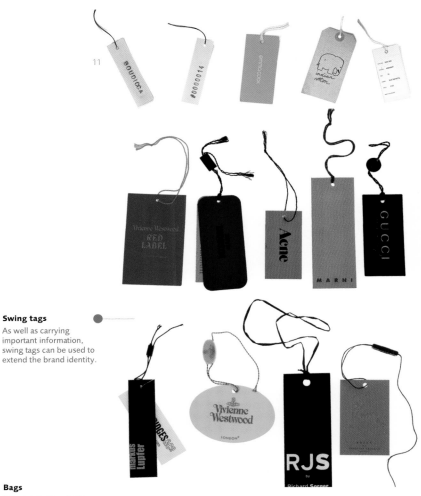

11

Promoting a collection

Think carefully about what you are trying to say about yourself as a designer or company. It is very important to stand apart from the other brands and designers with whom you are in competition. You can make yourself look far more established than you are through meticulous planning and design. Get garment labels woven up and swing tags made. Have a business card printed up – these will prove useful for all the networking that you will need to do, and are also essential at fabric trade fairs. If you need to work from home to save money, having a separate phone line will make you seem far more professional. Make sure that you have an answer phone too as it is very important that people can contact you easily.

Think about producing a website, but be careful when designing this – it is far better to produce a stylish, easily navigable one than a poorly and quickly produced one just for the sake of having an Internet presence. Wait until you can afford to create one properly. Don't try to sell your own goods on the Internet until you are well established and have lots of knowledge of selling online; it's a complicated business. Remember: you are a fashion designer, not an IT specialist! A sustainable fashion brand will take many years to build.

11 **Swing tags**
As well as carrying important information, swing tags can be used to extend the brand identity.

12 **Bags**
Bags are another form of promotion for a brand.

12

• 1 Research
• 2 Design
• 3 Fabrics and techniques
• 4 Construction
• 5 Developing a collection

Branding

A brand is made up of a mixture of elements, including a name, product, designer, quality, packaging, labelling and the 'X' factor of how it is perceived by the public. Some elements are more important to certain brands. With Levi's®, you might think of quality denim jeans and the big, worn, leather-like label. With Jean Paul Gaultier, you perhaps think of the designer's personality and humorous, experimental fashion. The name 'Prada' reflects an expensive high-quality design and product. The best brands are those with a strong, enduring identity.

Branding is the communication of the brand identity to the target customer, which includes the ticketing, labelling and the venue where the brand is sold. The branding of a garment is an integral part of the design of a garment; it is the part of a collection that remains consistent from season to season.

All fashion brands have a label for identification, usually positioned in the back neck of a garment so that they can be seen on the hanger in-store. Labels radically differ in terms of the font, colour or fabric used – even how they are stitched into the garment varies. All of these elements reflect directly on the designer. Garments also have a swing tag that is attached in store; it has the designer's name on it and the size and style number of the product, along with the retail price. Fashion garments are packaged after purchase and are usually presented in a bag; this is an important form of promotion for stores, and sometimes becomes a desirable object in itself.

1 **Garment labels**

The branding of a garment – here shown through a selection of labels – is an integral part of the design of a garment.

1

Boutiques

Designers with the finance to open their own boutique or store have the opportunity to present their clothes to the customer in their purest form. They can merchandise and display their garments exactly how they want. They can package their goods exclusively and train their staff to sell the collection perfectly. Stores that do this successfully offer the customer a total experience as soon as they walk into the store. It is therefore important that the shop is in the right location to reflect the appropriate image of the brand.

Prada used architect Rem Koolhaas/OMA to design their Los Angeles store. It has no signage on the front of the store – in fact, it has no frontage at all, but opens out directly onto the street, with nothing to protect the garments from the outside. The store looks more like a gallery than a fashion boutique.

In 2004, Comme des Garçons opened the first of their 'guerrilla' or pop-up stores in Berlin; these open in an underground area of a city, normally in a derelict building with no signage, and news of the store is then spread virally or by word of mouth. Each store trades only for a limited period of time before closing and moving on to another city.

The Internet

Having a website gives a fashion company a strong and easily accessible presence in the fashion market. It provides information about the brand, including a profile of the designer, images of the recent collection and a list of stockists. Customers are able to purchase goods easily and efficiently. When selling on the Internet, think carefully about delivery times to the customer as well as about how to manage returned goods.

2–4 **Marni store**
Marni's London store, designed by Sybarite, opened in 2003. This store has a modern, clean, pod-like feel. Highly designed curves and smooth forms lead you in and through the shop.

Selling lifestyle

In order to increase profitability, larger brands produce different products as an offshoot of their original fashion line, thereby creating a lifestyle for the consumer to buy into at various points and levels. Many fashion designers and companies now produce their own handbags, luggage, small leather goods, shoes, watches, jewellery, ties and scarves, eyewear, perfumes, cosmetics, skincare products and home accessories. Versace, Paul Smith, Prada and Gucci are examples of designers selling lifestyle. Armani opened their first Armani hotel in Dubai in 2010.

Some brands have also developed diffusion lines that are marginally cheaper and target a younger customer than do the mainline collections. McQueen launched his diffusion line McQ in Milan at the Autumn/Winter 2006 Milan fashion week. Chloé's second line is called See by Chloé; Marc Jacobs's diffusion line is called Marc by Marc Jacobs; Dolce & Gabbana's second line, D&G, which was launched in 1994, sadly closed in 2011.

Many designers also develop ranges for high-street stores. These ranges can be very lucrative for the designer, as well as attracting customers to the high-street store. It is a clever move by the designer to capitalize on the success of the name of a store to make more money. The product will share similarities to the designer's main line, but will be produced using cheaper fabrics and techniques, which then make the product more affordable. Some stores have produced a series of designer collections in this way. H&M, for instance, have collaborated with an impressive roster of designers to date, including Karl Lagerfeld, Stella McCartney, Versace, Lanvin, Jimmy Choo, Roberto Cavalli, Comme des Garçons, Sonia Rykiel, Matthew Williamson and Marni.

5

LOLA
MARC JACOBS

KARLIE PHOTOGRAPHED BY JUERGEN TELLER   LOLAMARCJACOBS.COM   THE NEW FRAGRANCE FOR WOMEN

5 **Marc Jacobs ad campaign**
A Marc Jacobs perfume ad, part of a series featuring models and celebrities photographed by artist Juergen Teller.

6

Relaunching brands

In true fashion-cyclic style, a flagging existing brand can be refreshed and relaunched. A team of experts and designers are brought in to rebrand, redesign and successfully promote the brand to a younger and more fashion-aware clientele.

In 1997, Burberry brought in Rose Marie Bravo as chief executive to make the brand younger and more accessible. She employed designer Christopher Bailey to successfully design the collections and commissioned a new advertising campaign featuring Kate Moss to promote the new clothes. Similarly, Tom Ford joined the struggling Gucci brand and turned it into a directional fashion company and a super brand once again.

Balenciaga employed Nicolas Ghesquière in the same year to introduce the brand to a younger, affluent market. Balenciaga, which was once one of the top couture houses in Paris, is now once again a very influential fashion house.

'You've got to know the rules before you can break them.'

Alexander McQueen

6   Balenciaga
Balenciaga rebranded to appeal to a younger market; from the Spring/Summer 2012 collection.

The Fundamentals of Fashion Design   183

In fashion:
Winni Lok, Calvin Klein

What is your job title?

Senior knitwear designer at Calvin Klein Collection, based in New York.

Please describe your job

I oversee all of the knitwear and cut and sew collections, which is eight collections per year for each area, and I work across both the commercial and runway collections.

My role involves everything from sourcing yarn, to stitch and fabrication developments, designing and fittings, to final sign-offs of all garment styles. However, my main objective is to try and create modern and forward-thinking designs, which push innovative techniques; and I work very closely with Francisco Costa, who is the Creative Director, and the wovens team in creating this vision for the house.

Fashion file

Upon graduating, Winni Lok went on to consult for Hussein Chalayan, Montana and Aquascutum. In 2005, she became head of design at Whistles in London, overseeing knitwear. In 2008, she moved to Nicole Farhi, London to become head of knitwear. Currently, Winni works as head of knits and sweaters for Calvin Klein Collection, New York.

Who else have you worked for?

Nicole Farhi, Whistles, Aquascutum, Montana, Hussein Chalayan and Marcus Constable. I had my own label for eight years, which was both men's and womenswear.

What was your career path to your current job?

Initially, I studied for a BA at Liverpool John Moores University and then undertook an MA at Central Saint Martins, London, UK. Up until my move to New York, I was also a visiting lecturer at Central Saint Martins on BA Fashion Knitwear and the External Assessor at Middlesex University on the BA Fashion course.

What do you do on an average day?

No two days are ever the same but if I am in New York, then it begins with speaking to or emailing my product manager in Milan, before organizing what needs to be done with my assistant. Then it's anything from designing, fitting or meetings about the collection. As I work across all collections, my days are extremely busy! I travel a lot too: Florence for Pitti Filati (the yarn fair) twice a year; we have an office in Milan, so we have fittings there too; and then research trips to say, London.

What are your normal working hours?

I work extremely long hours – up to 14-hour days when the studio calendar requires it. And there are also the weeks leading up to the show, so it is essentially a seven days a week job.

What essential qualities are needed for your job?

The sheer love of doing what you do, vision, positive energy and enthusiasm – and you need to be super organized. You also need to have an eye for the finer detail.

How creative a job do you have?

Extremely. The creative director is keen that developments and new techniques are constantly being sourced and pushed creatively. This means that there are no boundaries in what I want to do. I work with a couple of sample units in New York, and I might develop swatches with them or make garments for the show. We might also work with freelance designers in creating stitches, new fabrications, print developments, trims....

What kind of team do you work with?

I have an assistant and a production developer based in Milan, who works directly with our factories there to make sure that we get what we want. We work as an extremely tight unit, and it's really important for me that there is good communication and a rapport between us all. Then there is the wovens design team, a fabric buyer, a product developer and obviously I work closely with Francisco too.

What is the best part of your job?

That there really are no boundaries in what I want to develop initially for the collections, which is amazing! And that I am lucky enough to work with a wealth of creative people in developing ideas and techniques – the resources available to us are really quite incredible. Even though I have to juggle several projects at the same time, I get a real adrenaline buzz out of it all!

And the worst?

The long, long (at times, stressful) hours.

1

2

1–2 **Autumn/Winter 2012**
Key looks from the Calvin
Klein Autumn/Winter
2012 collection.

Developing a collection exercises

We have explored in this chapter how fashion garments can be categorized in many different ways. It is important to know what category of the market you are designing for and to identify who your target market is.

Designing a collection is one thing, but deciding how you promote it might make all the difference to whether it succeeds or fails. The branding and image of a company is very important in fashion. Let's now take a look at the steps that we might take in order to brand a new fashion label.

1–2 **Levi's® campaign**

Images from a Levi's® campaign photographed by Kent Baker, which rely on the viewer's familiarity with the brand identity rather than the overt use of logos.

Exercise 1

In this exercise, you will develop the brand look. To start with, do some preliminary research into fashion brands that interest you. What kind of products do these brands sell? How do they promote themselves? What is their 'look'?

- Think about the kind of brand that you want to create. What is its genre? What is the product range (is it high-end couture, denim or maybe childrenswear)? Consider your target market. Who will be interested in your garments? What kind of people are they? What do they look like? What images do they respond to?

- Now, put together two outfits that express the look of your brand. These could be sourced from thrift stores, second-hand shops or from garments that you have made yourself. Next, do some detailed research into different styles of fashion photography used for look books, web looks and magazine spreads. How are the models placed in their setting? Are they styled in groups or individually? Does the photographer work with interesting colours or layouts? Put together a moodboard of your research.

- Think about the kind of model you will use. Will they look good in the outfits that you have designed? Will they relate to your target market? Do some research into hair and make-up styling. Where will you take the photographs? Will you choose a location that your target market can relate to or aspire to? Or will you choose a studio shoot? Make sure that the hair, make-up and location don't overpower the clothes.

- Select the two shots that best express the 'look' of the brand from your shoot.

Exercise 2

Now you will set about creating a name and graphic design for your brand. What is your brand called? Does the name have longevity or will you get bored of it quickly? Do some research into branding ideas, graphics, fonts, ticketing and labelling. Look both at existing examples in fashion and also at the branding of other products. Create a moodboard to explore your findings.

- From your research and with the two 'looks' that you have photographed, create a graphic design that can be used for all the promotional activities of your new fashion brand. Will you use both text and an image, or just text? Think about font, style, size, colour and layout. Remember: the branding that you are creating here should not be specific to a certain season or collection; it needs to last for the lifetime of the brand.

- Incorporate the graphic that you created into the design of a fabric label for both the back neck of a garment and for a swing tag (which is put on a garment for retail). Think about the fabrication that you are using. What is the paper quality? Is the text printed or stitched?

Exercise 3

Finally, you need to incorporate this work into your look book. Take the two photographic images that you selected in the second exercise and, using a digital application, carefully lay out the images and the designed brand label as a double-page spread that can then be added into a look book.

▶ In context:
Maison Martin Margiela

In this chapter, we have looked briefly at branding and its importance for a fashion company. Maison Martin Margiela was founded in 1988 by Martin Margiela and is a fashion company with a very strong branding concept based on anonymity – from the labels on the garments to the styling of the models on the catwalk.

Maison Martin Margiela is essentially a conceptual fashion brand; it does not try to follow or set seasonal fashion trends. As a brand, it does not try to reinvent itself each season, but each new collection rather presents a development of sophisticated ideas. The product is of a high quality and this is reflected in its price; however, there are many product lines available featuring different concepts at various price points.

The Margiela product lines are identified through their labelling. The original label for the mainline collection is a white, blank, cotton tab, attached to the garment with four white stitches, one in each corner. In unlined garments, such as a jumper, the four stitches can be seen at the back neck when the jumper is worn.

Another label was introduced in 1997, with a numbering system to identify product lines. This label is also made of white cotton but has the numbers 0–23 printed in black on it, of which one number is circled according to the line that the product belongs to in the Margiela collection.

Product lines have evolved over time with new ones introduced periodically. In 1997, line 6 was created, which presented a complementary vision of femininity. This line then evolved into MM6 in 2004, which is less conceptual and more casual than the main line, with the creation of day-to-day basic pieces.

Further lines have since been created as follows:

- line 22 – comprising shoes for women, introduced in 1998 (men's were included in 2005)
- line 10 – a collection for men, which was introduced in 1998
- line 4 – a wardrobe for women, introduced in 2003
- line 14 – a wardrobe for men, introduced in 2004 to complement line 10
- line 11 – accessories for men and women, introduced in 2005
- line 8 – eyewear, introduced in 2007 with the first style named 'incognito'
- line 12 – fine jewellery, introduced in 2008
- line 3 – fragrances, introduced in 2010 with the perfume 'untitled'
- line 13 – new white objects, introduced in 2011
- line 0 artisanal – which takes objects and recrafts them; the label is sewn, embossed or stamped onto the product in whatever manner suits the product best.

The concept of anonymity is key to the Martin Margiela brand and Margiela himself has maintained an extremely low profile throughout his career. He has never had his picture taken and always remained backstage after his shows. All media contact was dealt with via fax and email from the house of Maison Martin Margiela – all replies being answered in the first person plural rather than being signed off by the man himself.

The models used within the catwalk shows or look books usually have their eyes blocked out, either with hair, make-up, tape or a shroud. Sometimes, their anonymity is achieved post-production with the top of the picture cut off above their nose or their eyes blanked out manually with black marker pen.

Stores are located off main high streets in inconspicuous areas; often, there are no clothes in the window, so the customer really has to seek the store out. The shops follow an all-white theme and the objects within them are often whitewashed or covered in white cotton or muslin; this works to effectively create a blank canvas for the clothes themselves.

Margiela also plays with the idea of trompe l'oeil, using photographs of eighteenth-century interiors within the stores as a way of directly referencing history but with a modern interpretation. The shop assistants wear white work-coats or 'blouses blanches', which are inspired by the work-coats worn at Parisian couturiers' ateliers. Packaging for the products is monochrome and logo-free, thereby completing the overarching concept and theme of anonymity which distinguishes the Margiela brand.

Martin Margiela himself has since left the company but because the brand concept is so strong, the fashion house successfully continues to trade as Masion Martin Margiela.

1 2

1–2 **Spring/Summer 2012**
Key looks from the Spring/
Summer 2012 Maison
Martin Margiela collection.
The concept of anonymity,
which is characteristic of
the brand, is expressed
through the obscured eyes
of the models.

Appendix

This book has examined the fundamental elements of fashion design and explored what happens to a collection once it has been made. It has introduced the process of research through to design, explored the basic properties of fabrics, treatments and decoration, and discussed the basic principles of pattern cutting and construction. Fashion design is essentially a combination of all of these elements.

A good designer needs to understand his or her methodology and be able to communicate ideas to others. He or she needs to have an understanding of the properties and the potential uses of fabric, along with some knowledge of how to make clothes. Designers cannot work in isolation and need to involve people in the process from other areas of the fashion industry in order to achieve success; a good designer is not necessarily the best publicist or stylist too!

The way to improve as a designer is through practice and repetition, which will thereby increase your knowledge and understanding of clothes. It is also important to get feedback about your work from someone working within the fashion industry. This may be from tutors or other designers, but it is essential to a designer's growth. Combine this with as many internships as you are able to undertake. This will improve your knowledge and understanding of the fashion industry and your work experience is something to add to your CV.

It will take some time to discover who you are as a designer, but once you do, embrace that person. As with any creative industry, fashion is about individuality. You will succeed as an independent designer, or be employed in the fashion industry, because of what you and you alone, can supply. Never be afraid to experiment and to challenge convention. Fashion involves – and needs – constant change; without innovation it would be doomed to simply repeat trends over and over and so would devour itself, as can sometimes be seen in its less inspired moments. Become knowledgeable of ethical issues within the fashion industry – as this is becoming a huge growth area. Work out which ones are important to you and try where possible to apply them to your practice.

We hope that you find much within this book to inspire you and to return to, as much as we have been inspired in creating it.

We hope you enjoy your future career in fashion!

Bibliography

A History of Costume in the West
François Boucher
Thames & Hudson, 1966 (paperback), 1996

Alexander McQueen: Savage Beauty
Andrew Bolton
Metropolitan Museum of Art, New York, Yale
University Press, 2011

Animals: 1,419 Copyright-Free Illustrations
of Mammals, Birds, Fish, Insects, etc.
(Ed.) Jim Harter
Dover Publications Ltd., 1980

Balenciaga Paris
(Ed.) Pamela Golbin
Thames & Hudson, 2006

Chanel
Harold Koda and Andrew Bolton
Metropolitan Museum of Art, New York, in
association with New Haven and London,
Yale University Press, 2005

Comme des Garçons
France Grand
Thames & Hudson, 1998

Designer Fact File
Caroline Coates
DTI and The British Fashion Council, 1997

Extreme Beauty: The Body Transformed
Harold Koda
Metropolitan Museum of Art, New York, Yale
University Press, 2001

Fabric Dyeing and Printing
Kate Wells
Conran Octopus, 2000

Fashion Brands: Branding Style from
Armani to Zara
Mark Tungate
Kogan Page Ltd, 2005

Fashion Design
Sue Jenkyn Jones
Laurence King Publishing, 2002

Fashion: The Collection of the Kyoto
Costume Institute: A History from the
18th to the 20th Century
Akiko Fukai
Taschen, 2002

Fashioning Fabrics: Contemporary
Textiles in Fashion
Sandy Black
Black Dog Publishing, 2006

Galliano
Colin McDowell
Weidenfeld & Nicolson, 1997

Haute Couture
Richard Martin and Harold Koda
The Metropolitan Museum of Art,
New York, 1995

How Fashion Works: Couture,
Ready to Wear and Mass Production
Gavin Wadell
Blackwell Science (UK), 2004

Isabella Blow
Martina Rink
Thames & Hudson, 2010

Jean Paul Gaultier
Farid Chenoune
Thames & Hudson, 1996

Lanvin
Dean L. Merceron
Rizzoli, 2007

Leigh Bowery: Looks
Fergus Greer
Violette Editions, 2002

Leigh Bowery: The Life and
Times of an Icon
Sue Tilley
Hodder & Stoughton, 1997

Maison Martin Margiela,
20: The Exhibition
Bob Verhelst and Kaat Debo
MoMu, 2008

Mastering Fashion Buying and
Merchandising Management
Tim Jackson and David Shaw
Palgrave McMillan, 2000

Men: A Pictorial Archive from
Nineteenth-Century Sources
(Ed.) Jim Harter
Dover Publications Ltd., 1980

Radical Fashion
(Ed.) Claire Wilcox
V&A Publications, 2001

Sample: 100 Fashion Designers – 010 Curators
Phaidon, 2005

Spectres: When Fashion Turns Back
Judith Clark
V&A Publications, 2005

The Art of Knitting
Françoise Tellier-Loumagne
Thames & Hudson, 2005

The Marchesa Casati: Portraits of a Muse
Scot D. Ryersson and Michael Orlando Yaccarino
Abrams, 2009

The New Boutique: Fashion and Design
Neil Bingham
Merrell Publishers Ltd, 2005

Victorian Fashions and Costumes
from Harper's Bazaar 1867–1898
(Ed.) Stella Blum
Dover Publications Ltd., 1974

Vivienne Westwood
Claire Wilcox
V&A Publications, 2005

Vivienne Westwood: An Unfashionable Life
Jane Mulvagh
Thames & Hudson, 1997

Further resources

Fashion schools

Belgium

Royal Academy of Fine Arts
Belgium
Fashion Department
Artesis Hogeschool Antwerpen
Nationalestraat 28/3
B–2000 Antwerp
www.antwerp-fashion.be

France

ESMOD
12 Rue de la Rochefoucauld
75009 Paris
www.esmod.com

Studio Berçot
29 rue des Petites-Écuries
F-75010 Paris
www.studio-bercot.com

Parsons School of Design
14 rue Letellier
75015 Paris
www.parsons-paris.com

Institut Français de la Mode
(postgraduate studies only)
36 quai d'Austerlitz
75013 Paris
www.ifm-paris.com

Germany

ESMOD
International University of
Art for Fashion
Görlitzer Str.51
10997 Berlin
www.esmod.de

ESMOD
International Fashion School
Fraunhofer Str. 23 h
D-80469 Munich
www.esmod.de

Italy

Istituto Marangoni
Via Pietro Verri 4
20121 Milan
www.istitutomarangoni.com

Domus Academy
Via Pichi 18
20143 Milan
www.domusacademy.it

Accademia di Costume e Moda
Via della Rondinella 2
00186 Rome
www.accademiacostumeemoda.it

Japan

Bunka Fashion College
3-22-1 Yoyogi
Shibuya-ku
Tokyo 151-8522
www.bunka-fc.ac.jp

Joshibi University of Art and
Design
1-49-8 Wada
Suginami- ku
Tokyo 166-8538
www.joshibi.ac.jp

Kobe Design University
8-1-1 Gakuennishi-machi
Nishi-ku
Kobe 651-2196
www.kobe-du.ac.jp

Vantan Design Institute
1-9-14 Ebisu-minami
Shibuya-ku
Tokyo 150-0022
www.vantan.com

The Netherlands

Gerrit Rietveld Academie
Frederik Roeskestraat 96
1076 ED Amsterdam
www.gerritrietveldacademie.nl
ArtEZ Hogeschool voor de

Kunsten
Onderlangs 9
6812 CE Arnhem
www.artez.nl

Hogeschool voor de Kunsten
Utrecht
Ina. Boudier-Bakkerlaan 50
3582 VA Utrecht
www.hku.nl

Spain

Istituto Europeo di Design
Torrent de L'olla 208
08012 Barcelona
and
Calle Larra 14
28004 Madrid
www.ied.es

ISA Academias de Moda
Escuela International de Diseno y
Moda
Calle Andrés Mellado 6
28015 Madrid
www.academiasisa.com

UK

Central Saint Martins College of
Art and Design
School of Fashion and Textiles
Granary Building
1 Granary Square
London, N1C 4AA
www.csm.arts.ac.uk

Middlesex University
School of Arts
Hendon Campus
The Burroughs
London, NW4 4BT
www.mdx.ac.uk

Kingston University
Faculty of Art, Design and Music
Knights Park
Grange Road
Kingston Upon Thames
Surrey, KT1 2QJ
www.kingston.ac.uk

Ravensbourne
6 Penrose Way
Greenwich Peninsula
London, SE10 0EW
www.rave.ac.uk

London College of Fashion
20 John Prince's Street
London, W1G 0BJ
www.fashion.arts.ac.uk

The Royal College of Art
Kensington Gore
London, SW7 2EU
www.rca.ac.uk

USA

Fashion Institute
of Technology (FIT)
227 W. 27th St. New York,
NY 10001-5992
www.fitnyc.edu

Parsons The New School
for Design
66 Fifth Avenue, New York,
NY 10011
www.newschool.edu

Pratt Institute
Brooklyn Campus
200 Willoughby Avenue
Brooklyn
NY 11205
www.pratt.edu

Academy of Art University
79 New Montgomery St
San Francisco
CA 94105-3410
www.academyart.edu

Webography

Online magazines

The following online magazines feature up-to-date fashion information and interesting moving image fashion features:

www.dazeddigital.com

www.showstudio.com

www.vogue.com/www.vogue.co.uk

www.style.com

Catwalk shows

For information on catwalk shows from graduate to designer, look at these websites:

www.gfw.org.uk

www.londonfashionweek.co.uk

www.catwalking.com

www.mbfashionweek.com

www.modeaparis.com

Ethical topics

Interesting ethical issues around fashion and lifestyle can be found on the following websites:

www.ethicalfashionforum.com

www.theecologist.org

www.fashioninganethicalindustry.org

Trend forecasting

For exciting trend information for fashion and design visit these:

www.wgsn.com

www.trendland.net

Technical innovations

This website is good for new technical innovations including fashion and textiles:

www.wired.com

Trade fairs

For information on the main biannual fabric fair in Paris visit:

www.premierevision.com

Textiles

For textile information, see:

www.thewoolroom.com

www.cottoninc.com

Glossary

Bias – the bias is at 45 degrees to the warp and weft of a fabric. A garment can be cut on the bias to give it a characteristic drape and elasticity.

Colour palette – a group of colours that are selected to work in combination.

Dart – sewn-in folds (that can be incorporated into seams) which give a flat piece of cloth three dimensions and so add fit or shape to the body.

Deconstructed – the reworking of an existing garment, or development of a new garment, where the seams are on the outside or the linings are removed, so giving a rough, unfinished look. Within tailoring, it also implies a garment that has little construction, for a softer look.

Haute couture – haute couture garments are made to fit an individual customer and are very expensive as the couturier uses both the most expensive fabrics and highly skilled artisans.

Look book – documents a collection and is a valuable selling and promotional tool. Images are usually styled to represent the designer's 'look' or concept for the collection.

Muse – a person, celebrity or model who is used as inspiration for a designer.

Quilting – a sewing method applied to layers of material in order to create a thicker, padded fabric.

RTW (Ready To Wear) – high-end collections that are designed for a wide range of clientele, unlike haute couture.

Seam – a seam is created when two or more pieces of fabric are joined together.

Selvedge – the edge of the warp of a fabric that naturally stops the sides from unravelling or fraying.

Silhouette – the outline shape of an outfit or collection.

SKU – a Stock-Keeping Unit is a number or code used to identify each unique product or item for sale in a store or other business.

Stand – a bust or a mannequin in the form of a man, woman or child, used for fitting, sizing or draping.

Thread – a length of continuous fibre used for stitching, it can be used for the construction of a garment or for decorative purposes. Thread can come in various weights and fibre, the choice of which depends on its use. Heavyweight nylon would be best to construct a workwear garment, whereas fine silk would be appropriate for decorative embroidery.

Toile – is French for cloth. 'Toile' in fashion terms describes a mock-up of an actual garment. It is made in a cheaper fabric – often calico (an unbleached, cotton fabric, in French known as *toile de coton*) to check fit and make.

Top-stitching – stitching that can be seen on the outside of a garment; it can be used for decorative purposes or to reinforce a seam.

Warp – lengthwise yarns that are stretched on a loom as the base structure of a piece of fabric.

Weft – yarns that are woven at 90 degrees to the warp in order to create a length of fabric. The way in which the warp and weft are woven together produces a variety of fabrics.

Working drawings – also called technical drawings, specifications (specs), or flats – these are linear drawings of a garment (shown as if laid out flat), showing both front and back details and accurate proportions. They are primarily used to communicate the design accurately to a pattern cutter and manufacturer.

Yarn – a length of continuous fibre used for weaving, knitting or crocheting.

Index

Index

Picture credits

Bronwen Marshall: 6–7, 15, 20, 22, 60

©Vivienne Westwood: 11

John-Gabriel Harrison: 17, 59

Catwalking.com: 18, 32–33, 34–35, 45, 50–51, 54–55, 56, 70–71, 72–73, 97, 99, 114–115, 129, 146–149, 152–153, 155, 158–159, 164, 166, 175, 183, 185, 189

Dover Publications Ltd: 19, 40–41, 80

Photography by Andrew Perris, APM Studios, andrew@apmstudios.co.uk: 19, 48, 52–53, 91, 94, 106, 111–113, 120–121, 125, 126–127, 128, 132–133, 134–135

Panda Parker: 20, 31, 59, 64, 69

Stuart Chapman: 21

Stephania Testa: 21

Sally Kite Norman: 23, 38–39

Bénédicte Zuccarelli: 24, 57, 61, 172

Kimberley Crampton: 25, 58, 60 (© Avant-Garde Studio LTD)

Louise Gray: 26–29 (photography: Antonio Salgado ©Jab Promotions)

V&A Images: 42–43 (©Victoria and Albert Museum, London)

Collection Groninger Museum (photographer: Peter Tahl): 44, 49, 130–131

Buket Ockay: 57

Rupal Patel: 57, 64

Richard Gray: 62–63

Peter Jensen: 67 (photography ©Tim Gutt), 81 (photography ©Autumn de Wilde), 171

Elena Rendina: 76–77 (©Elena Rendina)

Eppie Conrad: 78 (©Laura Jane Vest; ©Eppie Conrad)

Kuyichi: 79

Winni Lok: 80

Virginia James: 83 (www.wraplondon.com and www.poetryfashion.com)

Collection of the Kyoto Costume Institute: 85 (photography ©Richard Haughton)

Adidas: 86, 163 (©Adidas)

Studio XO Limited: 88 (commissioned by Rogier Van Der Heide, design director for Philips Lighting, and B. Åkerlund, stylist for the Black-Eyed Peas)

Sibling: 92–93, 167 (photography ©Thomas Giddings)

Kaoru Oshima: 95 (photography ©José Manuel Arguelles)

The D'Arcy Collection, Communications Library of University of Illinois: 96

Michael Kampe: 101 (designer: Michael Kampe; photography of exploded parka shot ©Soonhyun Choi)

Stefanie Nieuwenhuyse: 103 (corset on hanger ©Stefanie Nieuwenhuyse, photography ©Lucas Seidenfaden for Vauxhall Fashion Scout; corset modelled: photography ©Ezzidin Alwan)

7 For All Mankind: 105, 109

Première Vision: 107

Rex Features: 46–47 (Party at Westway Studios (left) ©Eugene Adebari/Rex Features; Belinda Carlisle Party (right) ©Richard Young/ Rex Features), 116–117 (©Olycom SPA/Rex Features), 154 (©Rex Features)

J. Braithwaite & Co. Ltd.: 122–123

Boudicca: 52–53, 128, 138–141, 176 ©Boudicca; ('Nicole in dark lace', photography ©Justin Edward John Smith)

Emma Cook: 157

Colin McNair at John Varvatos: 160–161

Richard James: 165 (photography ©John Spinks)

Flora McLean: 167

Alan Humphrey Bennett, Bally: 168–169 (images 2–5 ©Bally)

Jamie Russon: 173

Justin Smith, Esquire: 174

Magic 2006: 177

Sybarite: 181

Advertising Archives: 182

Kent Baker: 186 (©Kent Baker)

All reasonable attempts have been made to trace, clear and credit the copyright holders of the images reproduced in this book. However, if any credits have been inadvertently omitted, the publisher will endeavour to incorporate amendments in future editions.

Acknowledgements and credits

We would like to thank (in no particular order) all the talented people who have contributed to and helped with this book:

Bronwen Marsahall, Rupal Patel, Panda Parker (www.pandaparker.com), Stuart Chapman, Buket Ockay, Bénédicte Zuccarelli, Sally Kite, Kimberley Crampton, Stephania Testa, Boudicca (Brian Kirkby and Zowie Broach), Peter Jensen, Louise Gray, Winni Lok, Richard Gray, John-Gabriel Harrison, Kristin Forss, J. Braithwaite & Co. Ltd., Chris Moore at www.catwalking.com, Patrik Fredrikson, Ian Stallard, Grace Woodward, Elena Rendina, Kuyichi, Eppie Conrad, Nancy Tilbury, Sid Bryan, Michele Manz, Virginia James, Kaoru Oshima, Shelley Fox, Michael Kampe, Stefanie Nieuwenhuyse, Flora McLean, Annie Ovcharenko, Emma Cook, Colin McNair, Alan Humphrey Bennett, Justin Smith at J Smith Esq., Jamie Russon, Kent Baker, Perry Hampton, Richard James, James Pretty, Toby Lamb and Olok Banerjee at Richard James Savile Row, Marten de Leuuw at the Groninger Museum, Rie Nii at the Kyoto Costume Institute, Julia Meyers and Rita Gonçalves at Adidas, Studio XO Limited, Fergus Greer and Michael Hoppen Gallery.

Thank you to our editors for all their hard work; Georgia Kennedy, Rachel Parkinson, and an especially huge thank you to Colette Meacher for her patience and all the hard work she has put in to make the book look so exciting.

Thank you also to the designer, Luke Herriott at Studio Ink.

Richard Sorger: thanks to Jenny – it's been a pleasure working with you again! I would also like to thank my husband Gareth Williams for his help, love and support. Thank you for making me so happy!

Jenny Udale: thanks Richard, 'til the next time! Thank you Mum for looking after my gorgeous baby Wilfred while I tackled this rewrite and love to Baz for your endless support and advice.

Lynne Elvins/Naomi Goulder

Working with ethics

The Fundamentals
of Fashion Design

Ethical:
aware-
ness/
reflect-
ion/
debate

The subject of ethics is not new, yet its consideration within the applied visual arts is perhaps not as prevalent as it might be. Our aim here is to help a new generation of students, educators and practitioners find a methodology for structuring their thoughts and reflections in this vital area.

AVA Publishing hopes that these **Working with ethics** pages provide a platform for consideration and a flexible method for incorporating ethical concerns in the work of educators, students and professionals. Our approach consists of four parts:

The **introduction** is intended to be an accessible snapshot of the ethical landscape, both in terms of historical development and current dominant themes.

The **framework** positions ethical consideration into four areas and poses questions about the practical implications that might occur. Marking your response to each of these questions on the scale shown will allow your reactions to be further explored by comparison.

The **case study** sets out a real project and then poses some ethical questions for further consideration. This is a focus point for a debate rather than a critical analysis so there are no predetermined right or wrong answers.

A selection of **further reading** for you to consider areas of particular interest in more detail.

Ethics is a complex subject that interlaces the idea of responsibilities to society with a wide range of considerations relevant to the character and happiness of the individual. It concerns virtues of compassion, loyalty and strength, but also of confidence, imagination, humour and optimism. As introduced in ancient Greek philosophy, the fundamental ethical question is *what should I do?* How we might pursue a 'good' life not only raises moral concerns about the effects of our actions on others, but also personal concerns about our own integrity.

In modern times the most important and controversial questions in ethics have been the moral ones. With growing populations and improvements in mobility and communications, it is not surprising that considerations about how to structure our lives together on the planet should come to the forefront. For visual artists and communicators it should be no surprise that these considerations will enter into the creative process.

Some ethical considerations are already enshrined in government laws and regulations or in professional codes of conduct. For example, plagiarism and breaches of confidentiality can be punishable offences. Legislation in various nations makes it unlawful to exclude people with disabilities from accessing information or spaces. The trade of ivory as a material has been banned in many countries. In these cases, a clear line has been drawn under what is unacceptable.

But most ethical matters remain open to debate, among experts and lay-people alike, and in the end we have to make our own choices on the basis of our own guiding principles or values. Is it more ethical to work for a charity than for a commercial company? Is it unethical to create something that others find ugly or offensive?

Specific questions such as these may lead to other questions that are more abstract. For example, is it only effects on humans (and what they care about) that are important, or might effects on the natural world require attention too?

Is promoting ethical consequences justified even when it requires ethical sacrifices along the way? Must there be a single unifying theory of ethics (such as the Utilitarian thesis that the right course of action is always the one that leads to the greatest happiness of the greatest number), or might there always be many different ethical values that pull a person in various directions?

As we enter into ethical debate and engage with these dilemmas on a personal and professional level, we may change our views or change our view of others. The real test though is whether, as we reflect on these matters, we change the way we act as well as the way we think. Socrates, the 'father' of philosophy, proposed that people will naturally do 'good' if they know what is right. But this point might only lead us to yet another question: *how do we know what is right?*

You
What are your ethical beliefs?

Central to everything you do will be your attitude to people and issues around you. For some people their ethics are an active part of the decisions they make every day as a consumer, a voter or a working professional. Others may think about ethics very little and yet this does not automatically make them unethical. Personal beliefs, lifestyle, politics, nationality, religion, gender, class or education can all influence your ethical viewpoint.

Using the scale, where would you place yourself? What do you take into account to make your decision? Compare results with your friends or colleagues.

Your client
What are your terms?

Working relationships are central to whether ethics can be embedded into a project and your conduct on a day-to-day basis is a demonstration of your professional ethics. The decision with the biggest impact is whom you choose to work with in the first place. Cigarette companies or arms traders are often-cited examples when talking about where a line might be drawn, but rarely are real situations so extreme. At what point might you turn down a project on ethical grounds and how much does the reality of having to earn a living affect your ability to choose?

Using the scale, where would you place a project? How does this compare to your personal ethical level?

01 02 03 04 05 06 07 08 09 10

01 02 03 04 05 06 07 08 09 10

Your specifications
What are the impacts of your materials?

In relatively recent times we are learning that many natural materials are in short supply. At the same time we are increasingly aware that some man-made materials can have harmful, long-term effects on people or the planet. How much do you know about the materials that you use? Do you know where they come from, how far they travel and under what conditions they are obtained? When your creation is no longer needed, will it be easy and safe to recycle? Will it disappear without a trace? Are these considerations the responsibility of you or are they out of your hands?

Using the scale, mark how ethical your material choices are.

Your creation
What is the purpose of your work?

Between you, your colleagues and an agreed brief, what will your creation achieve? What purpose will it have in society and will it make a positive contribution? Should your work result in more than commercial success or industry awards? Might your creation help save lives, educate, protect or inspire? Form and function are two established aspects of judging a creation, but there is little consensus on the obligations of visual artists and communicators toward society, or the role they might have in solving social or environmental problems. If you want recognition for being the creator, how responsible are you for what you create and where might that responsibility end?

Using the scale, mark how ethical the purpose of your work is.

01   02   03   04   05   06   07   08   09   10

01   02   03   04   05   06   07   08   09   10

One aspect of fashion design that raises an ethical dilemma is the way that clothes production has changed in terms of the speed of delivery of products and the now international chain of suppliers. 'Fast fashion' gives shoppers the latest styles sometimes just weeks after they first appeared on the catwalk, at prices that mean they can wear an outfit once or twice and then replace it. Due to lower labour costs in poorer countries, the vast majority of Western clothes are made in Asia, Africa, South America or Eastern Europe in potentially hostile and sometimes inhumane working conditions. It can be common for one piece of clothing to be made up of components from five or more countries, often thousands of miles apart, before they end up in the high-street store. How much responsibility should a fashion designer have in this situation if manufacture is controlled by retailers and demand is driven by consumers? Even if designers wish to minimize the social impact of fashion, what might they most usefully do?

Traditional Hawaiian feather capes (called 'Ahu'ula) were made from thousands of tiny bird feathers and were an essential part of aristocratic regalia. Initially they were red ('Ahu'ula literally means 'red garment') but yellow feathers, being especially rare, became more highly prized and were introduced to the patterning.

The significance of the patterns, as well as their exact age or place of manufacture is largely unknown, despite great interest in their provenance in more recent times. Hawaii was visited in 1778 by English explorer Captain James Cook and feather capes were amongst the objects taken back to Britain.

The basic patterns are thought to reflect gods or ancestral spirits, family connections and an individual's rank or position in society. The base layer for these garments is a fibre net, with the surface made up of bundles of feathers tied to the net in overlapping rows. Red feathers came from the 'i'iwi or the 'apapane. Yellow feathers came from a black bird with yellow tufts under each wing called 'oo'oo, or a mamo with yellow feathers above and below the tail.

Thousands of feathers were used to make a single cape for a high chief (the feather cape of King Kamehameha the Great is said to have been made from the feathers of around 80,000 birds). Only the highest-ranking chiefs had the resources to acquire enough feathers for a full-length cape, whereas most chiefs wore shorter ones which came to the elbow.

The demand for these feathers was so great that they acquired commercial value and provided a full-time job for professional feather-hunters. These fowlers studied the birds and caught them with nets or with bird lime smeared on branches. As both the *'i'iwi* and *'apapane* were covered with red feathers, the birds were killed and skinned. Other birds were captured at the beginning of the moulting season, when the yellow display feathers were loose and easily removed without damaging the birds.

The royal family of Hawaii eventually abandoned the feather cape as the regalia of rank in favour of military and naval uniforms decorated with braid and gold. The *'oo'oo* and the *mamo* became extinct through the destruction of their forest feeding grounds and imported bird diseases. Silver and gold replaced red and yellow feathers as traded currency and the manufacture of feather capes became a largely forgotten art.

Is it more ethical to create clothing for the masses rather than for a few high-ranking individuals?

Is it unethical to kill animals to make garments?

Would you design and make a feather cape?

Fashion is a form of ugliness so intolerable that we have to alter it every six months.

Oscar Wilde

AIGA
Design business and ethics
2007, AIGA

Eaton, Marcia Muelder
Aesthetics and the good life
1989, Associated University Press

Ellison, David
Ethics and aesthetics in European modernist literature:
from the sublime to the uncanny
2001, Cambridge University Press

Fenner, David E W (Ed)
Ethics and the arts:
an anthology
1995, Garland Reference Library of Social Science

Gini, Al and Marcoux, Alexei M
Case studies in business ethics
2005, Prentice Hall

McDonough, William and Braungart, Michael
Cradle to cradle:
remaking the way we make things
2002, North Point Press

Papanek, Victor
Design for the real world:
making to measure
1972, Thames and Hudson

United Nations Global Compact
The ten principles
www.unglobalcompact.org/AboutTheGC/TheTenPrinciples/index.htr